C000184425

THE MANAGEMENT OF CO

The Management of Construction Firms

Aspects of Theory

Edited by

Patricia Hillebrandt

and

Jacqueline Cannon

Foreword by W. D. Biggs

MACMILLAN

First edition 1989
Reprinted 1994

Published by
THE MACMILLAN PRESS LTD
Houndmills, Basingstoke, Hampshire RG21 2XS
and London
Companies and representatives
throughout the world

ISBN 0–333–41602–3 hardcover
ISBN 0–333–62761–X paperback

A catalogue record for this book is available
from the British Library.

Printed in Great Britain by
Antony Rowe Ltd
Chippenham, Wiltshire

To our children

Contents

List of Figures

List of Tables

Preface to the 1994 Reprint

In 1986 and 1987 when most of the work was carried out for the two books: *The Management of the Construction Firm: Aspects of Theory* and *The Modern Construction Firm*, the environment in which contractors were operating was one of expanding markets and rising profits. Contractors were increasing their turnover in response to boom conditions, banks were anxious to lend money, most construction companies were involved in property and housing and diversifying into other businesses in the UK and abroad, and all were optimistic about the future.

A third book in the series, *The Construction Company in-and-out of Recession*, which deals with the changes in the environment and the way in which companies have reacted to the worst recession in the construction industry since the Second World War, is to be published. Interviews conducted at the end of 1993 confirmed that companies had shrunk, were retreating into their 'core' businesses and in a few cases were concerned with whether they could survive at all over the period 1994 to 1995. The strategies of the companies in this recessionary environment contrast sharply with those of the earlier period. However, with hindsight it is clear that the seeds of some of the current problems were sown already in 1986 and 1987. The books together provide a unique insight into the dynamics of major construction firms.

Foreword

In 1981 the Science and Engineering Research Council allocated £1.4 million index linked for a specially promoted programme of research into construction management. The programme was to be coordinated by my colleague Roger Flanagan and myself under the guidance of a Steering Committee.

We started somewhat hesitantly – we had no real idea of the size of the research community, or the skills available within it. But it soon became clear that most researchers had trained (and were researching) in areas with a predominantly technical bias. But construction is not a particularly innovative process technologically – though this is perhaps changing. It is however a complex problem managerially, largely because of the many different skills required in both the design and construction phases. Our definition of 'management' is perhaps naive – the practical application of the social sciences – and it was clear that none of our then researchers had received formal training in the rich research methodologies of the social sciences.

Somewhat to our surprise the Steering Committee (mostly industrialists) agreed with our concern and we were encouraged to look more widely into the problems of management and to encourage the research teams that might tackle them. We are indebted to the Committee for this long term view.

Seven years on, and with interdisciplinary research being actively encouraged and supported, it seems hard to believe that for the Science and Engineering Council to be prepared to award grants to Departments of Sociology, Economics, etc. was quite a momentous step. Now it all seems so obvious.

Overall, I have found these interdisciplinary projects among the most interesting and rewarding, but it must be admitted that dissemination of the findings has not been easy. Academics have always tended to publish for their own peers and the pressure to do this has, over the last few years, been severe and even savage. Targeting a non-specialist audience is another matter.

The present work grew out of the interdisciplinary objectives and it links not only different academic disciplines but also, with the companion volume, it links theory and practice by selecting and interpreting those areas of theory relevant to the contracting company. It has been a great source of discovery for me to have been associated with it. By publishing in book form we hope that both specialist and non-specialist readers will find something of interest – hopefully of lasting interest.

Finally, of course, no one could work with Pat Hillebrandt and Jacquie Cannon and not be tempted to drop everything else and follow in the wake of their contagious enthusiasm. I am grateful for having been allowed the privilege.

W. D. BIGGS

Acknowledgements

The editors would like to thank first the authors who contributed to this volume, not only for producing the chapters which follow and for their support in the project as a whole, but also for bearing so patiently the requests to alter and amend their texts. Secondly they wish to express their appreciation to friends and colleagues for helpful support and comments at all stages of the project, in particular to John Bennett, Mark Casson, John Dunning, Norman Fisher, Roger Flanagan, Peter Lansley, Jamie Stevenson and Sir Peter Trench and, most importantly of all, to Bill Biggs who guided, cajoled and supported us so valiantly throughout the whole process of the study. Thirdly the book would not have been possible without the constant efforts of Sheila Rogers, the Secretary of the Department of Construction Management at Reading University, and her team. We thank them all.

PATRICIA M. HILLEBRANDT
JACQUELINE CANNON

Abbreviations and Acronyms

AGR	Advanced gas cooled reactor
BISS	Bartlett International Summer School
BoQ	Bill of quantities
CAD	Computer aided design
CAM	Computer aided management
CI/SfB	Construction Index/Samarbetskommitten för Byggnadsfragor (classification system authorised by CIB for structuring and filing of construction industry information)
CITB	Construction Industry Training Board
EBIT	(Total) earnings before interest and taxes
EPS	Earnings per share
ESRC	Economic and Social Research Council
FDI	Foreign direct investment
ILM	Internal labour market
KFS	Key factors of success
PBR	Payment by results
P/E	Profit/Equity
PIMS	Profit impact of marketing strategies
R & D	Research and development
ROCE	Return on capital employed
ROE	Return on equity
ROI	Return on investment
SWOT	Strengths, weaknesses, opportunities, threats
WIP	Work in progress
WORC	Work Organisation Research Centre (Aston)

Notes on the Contributors

Professor W. D. Biggs is Professor of Building Technology, University of Reading.

Professor Peter J. Buckley is Professor of Managerial Economics, University of Bradford Management Centre.

Mrs Jacqueline Cannon is Senior Visiting Research Fellow, Department of Construction Management, University of Reading and Visiting Professor at the University of Westminster.

Dr Peter Clark is Principal Investigator, Work Organisation Research Centre, University of Aston in Birmingham.

Dr Peter Enderwick is Lecturer in Economics, Queen's University, Belfast.

Professor Roger Flanagan is Professor, Department of Construction Management, University of Reading.

Dr Patricia M. Hillebrandt is Senior Research Fellow, Department of Construction Management, University of Reading.

Dr Steven Male is Lecturer in Construction Management, Heriot–Watt University.

Professor George Norman is Tyler Professor of Economics, University of Leicester.

Mr. William Ramsay is an Associate Fellow, Templeton College, Oxford.

Dr Howard Seymour is Building Analyst, Phillips & Drew.

Mr Robert Stocks is Lecturer in Construction Management, Heriot–Watt University.

Introduction

Patricia M. Hillebrandt and
Jacqueline Cannon

1 THE PROJECT

This book represents one half of a project on the strategic behaviour of large UK building and civil engineering contractors, all with some overseas experience. It offers a number of theoretical approaches from different disciplines which help to analyse and explain the decision making processes of large contracting firms. The project was undertaken at the University of Reading and funded by the SERC Specially Promoted Programme in Construction Management.

The project originated because it was thought that the way in which contracting firms operate had been largely neglected by researchers. There was a need to link relevant aspects of economics, management sociological and financial theories in investigating the way the industry functioned and to examine how relevant those theories seemed to be to the specific characteristics of contracting firms.

In the field of economics in particular the difficulties presented in the analysis of contracting firms by the characteristics of their products have long been recognised, but not explicitly examined in relation to the firms' actual behaviour.

The first task in the project was to select the areas for study. They are those of the chapters in this volume. The authors were selected, sometimes because of their special knowledge of the construction industry, but often because they were concerned in their work with a broader canvas of industry. The discussions which took place in the early stages of the process of writing and subsequently made a stimulating contribution to the preparation of the book. They bear witness to the richness and diversity of thinking which specialist disciplines can bring to the study of the contracting firm.

The second part of the project was to conduct a series of interviews with the principal decision makers in about twenty of the largest UK construction firms. The companion volume, *The Modern Construction Firm* is based on the results obtained from those interviews.

2 CHARACTERISTICS OF THE CONSTRUCTION INDUSTRY

The products of the construction industry have well-known characteristics, which differentiate them strongly from most other industries. Their location is fixed, their geographical distribution widespread, they are large, heavy, one-off and custom built, generally long lived and expensive.

Those characteristics go a long way to explain methods of production, and organisation, price determination, payment methods, financial decisions and controls, and an industrial structure unlike those met in other sectors. Hence the construction process generates management problems and opportunities at the level of the firm which may differ in scope, in scale, in time and in the type of appropriate solutions from those met in firms of other industries.

Because of the nature of the product the production process does not lend itself to the use of capital intensive methods. Hence the industry is very labour intensive. In addition, the fact that the demand for any type of product is not continuous in time or place, and that different inputs are required over the life of the project, leads to great difficulties in the long term employment of manpower. In the post war period, but essentially in the 1970s and 1980s this has led to a major shift away from direct often casual employment towards greater reliance on subcontractors.

The same factors explain why a site manager has both a specialist function and a general management role. On site, there are few routine procedures similar to those which are available because of the existence of a repetitive manufacturing process. Adequate numbers of high quality managers are thus the most important assets of a contracting firm. What the contracting firm is really selling is its management skills.

Low fixed capital assets mean that financial capital requirements for a contracting firm are low and, because of the peculiar pricing and payment system, the contractor is able to have a high positive cash flow. This factor, together with the importance of managers, has a profound influence on the strategy of contracting firms.

3 MANAGEMENT OF CHANGE

There is no chapter in this volume on the management of change. Yet it is clear from Section 2 above that the construction industry, more than almost any other, faces continuous and at times violent changes in work load, in work mix and in the method of managing the process. It is almost by definition changing its product all the time. Since each project is essentially different from previous ones, the whole management process undergoes continuous change. Moreover, over the life of the individual projects there is a constant change of emphasis on the relative importance of inputs and functions from the estimating and planning stage through site operations to commissioning.

In a sense, this whole book is about a firm's management of change – coping with changes in the environment and making adjustments to its strategy,[1] diversifying as necessary, modifying its international operations, altering its methods of employment of manpower, updating its approach to managers, changing its organisational structure and making constant adjustments to its financial and pricing policies.

Any contracting firm has to respond to the changing environment of the market place for projects and of the market for resources every time it tenders for a job. It is the nature and quality of its response, described in the companion volume, which determines the firm's success.

4 OUTLINE OF THE BOOK

Chapter 1 sets out the relevant theoretical elements of the economic analysis of firms, and shows how the characteristics of the industry make it difficult to apply those theories to the behaviour of construction firms. The uniqueness of most projects calls for complex organisational and managerial controls. In Chapter 2, William Ramsay brings out the interrelationships of firms' objectives, strategy and mission and the key strategic elements for success in the contracting business. The availability of funds from contracting operations gives opportunities for diversification as part of the firm's strategy. Chapter 3 by Jacqueline Cannon and Patricia Hillebrandt examines the opportunities and the factors which influence diversification policy.

The fact that the product sold by contracting firms is essentially management skills helps to explain the international context of the operations of large contracting firms. In Chapter 4, Howard Seymour examines construction within a framework of international production economics. Chapter 5, by Jacqueline Cannon and Patricia Hillebrandt, emphasises that some of the financial tenets relevant to other large firms are inapplicable to construction firms, and points to the consequences in terms of horizontal and vertical diversification choices.

The complexity of the construction product emphasises the need to concentrate on appropriate means of management. In Chapter 6, Peter Clark offers a sociological framework that may facilitate analysis of relationships between and within groups, while the focus of Chapter 7 by Steven Male and Robert Stocks is on the motivation of the individual manager and some of the ways in which he functions within the organisation.

In Chapter 8, Peter Buckley and Peter Enderwick deal with the management of construction manpower, which particularly relates to the problems of discontinuity mentioned above.

In Chapter 9, Roger Flanagan and George Norman explore the crucial area of pricing policy, where the one-off nature of projects precludes reliance on most of traditional pricing theory, with its focus on standardised products.

NOTE

1. See also the article by Lansley, P. R., 'Corporate Strategy and Survival in the UK Construction Industry', *Construction Management and Economics*, Vol. 5, No. 2 (Autumn 1987) pp. 141–55.

1 Theories of the Firm

Jacqueline Cannon and
Patricia M. Hillebrandt

1.1 THE ECONOMIC THEORY OF THE FIRM

The large firm is a phenomenon of the 20th century. At the time of the development of micro-economics, the typical firm was small and owner-controlled. The owner took risks backed by his own capital, and was accountable only to himself. Economists focused on such a firm, within markets where products were standardised, buyers and suppliers were large in number and well informed about the conditions prevailing in these markets, and where prices were set by the market forces. That is perfect competition.

The theory of the firm was thus based on the assumption that all decisions concerning the business were made by the owner of the firm, except that he had to accept, as the price for his product and inputs, that set by the interaction of market forces of demand and supply. In this model, it is efficiency in production which enables the firm's owner to earn a return on his investment, and his aim is profit maximisation.

The distinguishing feature of the traditional approach is that risk carrying, reward reaping and operational decision taking are all vested in one individual. He knows that *if* successful, the benefits will accrue to him alone. Traditional capitalism thus encourages the owner to minimise the costs of risk taking while maximising the efficiency of decision taking.

The perfect competition model of the firm assumes profit maximisation. It is based on the concept of marginalism – that is, the additional costs and revenues arising from the production of one more unit. The firm's production is profitable so long as the revenue from an extra unit is greater than the cost of producing it. The firm's profit therefore, continues to increase up to the point where the cost of the last unit produced is exactly met by the revenue which is generated: in other words, where marginal cost equals marginal revenue. To increase production beyond that point implies a

1

reduction in profits, since marginal revenue will then be lower than marginal cost and profits are no longer maximised.

In the 19th century this particular structure was overtaken by 'managerial capitalism', an economic system in which production was controlled by large joint stock companies. In developed economies, a significant percentage of output is now produced by large firms of that type, hence the separation between ownership and control: the shareholders own the firm, the managers control it.

The increase in industrial concentration led to the development of new approaches to the theory of the firm and where market conditions stray from perfect competition to oligopoly and monopoly and various other types of markets. In oligopoly, a small number of producers typically dominate the market for a product or group of products, while monopoly refers to a market where one producer holds a dominant position.

The main advantage of joint stock companies is that they overcome the major weakness of the owner-managed firm – namely, the restraint on scale. Since finance is the means to investment and hence growth, the fact that joint stock companies facilitate investment is a crucial feature of modern firms at the forefront of technological know-how and application. It is less important to contracting firms since they rely less on large physical assets than other industries. It is noteworthy that a considerable percentage of large UK contractors are still 'family firms', in the sense that majority shareholdings are held by groups of individuals, linked by family ties.

The pioneer writers on the separation of ownership and control, Berle and Means[1] noted that between 1929 and 1962, the share of net capital assets of all US manufacturing corporations held by the hundred largest corporations rose from 44 to 58 per cent. The traditional theory of the firm came under attack as it was found wanting in a number of ways. It was pointed out that, in the real world, firms did not behave as the theory suggested. Moreover, it was argued that the theory neglected many aspects of the modern firm's behaviour such as management planning and budgetary procedures, which are an integral part of firms' decision making.

1.2 MANAGERIAL ECONOMICS

Managerial economics attempts to overcome the weaknesses of the traditional theory by broadening its domain to all decisions within firms. Major contributions to the development of the discipline have been made by Simon, Baumol, Williamson and Marris.

In a seminal article published in 1959, Simon[2] drew attention to a number of specific criticisms levied at the assumption of profit maximisation. He suggested in particular that where ownership and management are divorced, those responsible for the latter may not seek to maximise profits. Moreover, even entrepreneurs themselves may not care to maximise profits, but might be content with satisfactory profits. According to Simon, firms might be trying 'to satisfice rather than to maximise'. He quotes the research work undertaken by Hall and Hitch[3] in support of his argument. In a series of interviews with businessmen, they found that they set prices by adding a standard mark-up to costs and were therefore not profit maximisers. In any case, Simon points out that entrepreneurs have limited knowledge and computational capacity and are therefore subject to 'bounded rationality'.

Baumol's[4] model eschews the assumption of maximising profits, which is replaced by the notion of sales revenue maximisation. The theory incorporates two criteria, rather than the single one of the traditional theory, for the assumption of sales maximisation is complemented by that of a satisfactory level of profits. Two particularly important conclusions can be drawn from Baumol's analysis. Firstly if a firm is faced with increasing costs, either they will be passed on to consumers through higher prices or they will be absorbed by the firm through, for example, lower expenditure which the firm can control. Advertising expenditure is such an area. Secondly, the sales maximisation model presumes that businessmen will prefer non-price competition.

Williamson[5] seeks an answer to the question of 'why organisations?' The one he offers is simple: because they lower transaction costs. Williamson's 'transactional paradigm' is based on the information cost of transactions. This model contrasts with the model of the firm put forward by Penrose[6] with its emphasis on economies of scale and economies of growth. Transaction costs may be defined as the costs involved in the process of buying and selling both goods and services, including manpower. They include, for example, the advertising costs of the search for manpower, the time taken in interviewing and in agreeing terms for employment. If the firm requires long term employment and therefore engages personnel on such a basis, these costs arise less frequently and are lower overall than where the firm engages personnel on an *ad hoc* basis and has therefore continually to seek information on the current market conditions for the various skills required, and on the availability of persons to provide the skills. The reason, according to Williamson, for the existence of organisations is that the information cost of transactions is internalised.

Where the transaction costs are internalised, they are thus supplementary to costs incurred directly by a firm in the purchase of inputs. The economic analysis of costs facing contracting firms has been fully treated by Hillebrandt while Gunnarson and Levitt[7] have examined the relevance of transaction costs to the construction industry.

Some transaction costs arise when transactions take place both within a market and within an organisation. Both markets and hierarchies within firms are suitable for the conduct of transactions, and the choice depends on what Williamson terms 'information impactedness'. This is defined as the situation where the true underlying circumstances of a transaction are known to some parties, but not to all.

Baumol, Williamson and Marris[8] view the technostructure of large organisations as essentially concerned with the survival of the organisation within which they operate. The personal interests of the technostructure are satisfied by the pursuit of growth and increase in size of the firm, subject to a minimum profit constraint required to keep shareholders happy.

Williamson recognised that within hierarchical organisations more complex structures are established than the two-level system met in firms with few products and of small size. The large multi-product firm usually has at least a three-tier system. The unitary structure (*U* form) is illustrated in Figure 1.1 and the multi-divisional structure

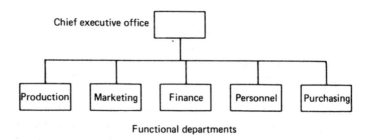

Figure 1.1 U-form organisation

Source: McGuinness, T., 'Markets and Managerial Hierarchies', in Clarke, R. and McGuinness, T., *The Economics of the Firm* (Oxford: Basil Blackwell, 1987) p. 54.

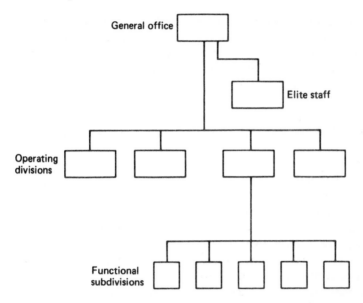

Figure 1.2 *M*-form organisation

Source: McGuinness, T., 'Markets and Managerial Hierarchies', in Clarke, R. and McGuinness, T., *The Economics of the Firm* (Oxford: Basil Blackwell, 1987) p. 56.

(*M* form) in figure 1.2. The *M* form was first introduced by large US industrial firms who found that the *U* form was unsuitable when they adopted a diversifying strategy.

Finally, Baumol[9] has put forward the concept of contestable markets as a suitable explanation for the behaviour of organisations. Barriers to entry,[10] and their height, determine the extent of the difficulties facing potential new entrants to a market. Contestable markets are those in which the danger of entry by potential competitors constrains the behaviour of existing producers even if there are only one or a few firms in the market. For a market to be contestable, barriers to entry must therefore be negligible.

It follows that in order to prevent profitable opportunities for entry, excess profits must be low and price setting and production sharing by existing suppliers must be efficient. The contracting industry, with its low capital requirements, has been suggested as an example of a contestable market. The concept is further commented upon in Chapter 9 on pricing policy.

Theories of the firm have altered their focus from the small

entrepreneurial business to large firms in an oligopolistic environment and to diversified corporations. Yet they still treat of firms
involved in processing standardised products, the sales of which are
influenced by advertising expenditures. It remains therefore inherently difficult to relate the economic structure, behaviour and
performance of contracting firms to theoretical models. The main
problem lies in the characteristics of the products of the industry and
particularly in their one-off nature and long gestation period.

1.3   THEORIES OF MANAGEMENT

There is no body of management theory in the way that there is an
economic theory of the firm, in which all the component parts are
interrelated in a total system. This is partly because originally
management theory was developed from a number of other disciplines or from experience of practical managers; though it is now an
academic subject in its own right yet it still consists of a number of
related but separate bodies of theory. These may be categorised as:
business strategy, organisation theory and the management of human
resources.

Business strategy includes the determination of long and short term
objectives of the firm and the means by which these objectives may
be achieved.[11] It must encompass financial and marketing strategies
and also diversification theory, though these three subjects also draw
heavily on other disciplines.

Organisation theory is concerned with the type of organisation or
structure which is most suited to the business of the firm, and it
overlaps with the management of human resources, especially in the
management style adopted by an organisation. It is a substantial area
of academic endeavour and has resulted in a number of different
approaches.[12] One of these is described in Chapter 6 on social
technology and structure. Other theories are touched on in Chapter 7
on managers and the organisation.

Lastly there has been much written on the management of human
resources,[13] including such subjects as leadership, motivation and the
psychology of group behaviour, all of which potentially merge in the
subject of personnel management, including education and training.
Much of the psychological and sociological work in this area is aimed
at understanding and analysing behaviour in various situations and
does *not* necessarily lead to statements of how people *should* be

managed. Parts of the theory are of great relevance for managing in contracting; those of particular relevance have been selected in Chapter 7 on managers and the organisation.

REFERENCES

1. Berle, A. A. and Means, C. G., *The Modern Corporation and Private Property* (New York: The Commerce Clearing House, 1932).
2. Simon, H. A., 'Theories of Decision Making in Economics and Behavioral Science', *American Economic Review*, Vol. 49 (1959) pp. 253–83.
3. Hall R. L. and Hitch, C. J., 'Price Theory and Business Behaviour', in Wilson, T. and Andrews, P. W. S. (eds), *Oxford Studies in the Price Mechanism* (Oxford: Oxford University Press, 1951).
4. Baumol, W. J., *Business Behaviour; Value and Growth* (New York: Macmillan, 1959, 1967).
5. Williamson, O. E., *Markets and Hierarchies: Analysis and Anti-trust Implications – A Study in the Economics of Internal Organisation* (New York: Free Press and Collier Macmillan, 1975).
6. Penrose, E. T., *The Theory of the Growth of the Firm* (Oxford: Basil Blackwell, 1959).
7. Hillebrandt, P. M., *Economic Theory and the Construction Industry* (London: Macmillan, 1974) and Gunnarson, S. and Levitt, R. E., 'Is a Building Construction Project a Hierarchy or a Market?', *Proceedings, Internet* (Summer 1982).
8. (Baumol (1959, 1967), (see note 4), Williamson (1975) (see note 5) and Marris, R. L., *The Economic Theory of Managerial Capitalism* (London: Macmillan; New York: Free Press, 1964).
9. Baumol, W. J., Panzar, J. C. and Willig, R. D., *Contestable Markets and the Theory of Industry Structure* (New York: Harcourt Brace Jovanovich, 1982).
10. Bain, J. S., *Barriers to New Competition: Their Character and Consequences in Manufacturing Industry* (Cambridge, Mass.: Harvard University Press, 1956).
11. See for example Ansoff, H. I., *Corporate Strategy* (New York: McGraw-Hill, 1968).
12. See for example Morgan, G., *Images of Organisation* (Beverley Hills: Sage, 1986), Woodward, J., *Industrial Organisation: Theory and Practice* (Oxford: Oxford University Press, 1965, 2nd edn 1980); Burns, T. and Stalker, G. M., *The Management of Innovation* (London: Tavistock, 1966, 2nd edn 1968); The Aston Group, including D. S. Pugh and John Child, in, for example, Chandler, A. D., *Strategy and Structure* (Cambridge Mass.: MIT Press, 1962).
13. See, for example, Hunt, J., *Managing People at Work* (London: McGraw Hill, 1981), Handy, C. B., *Understanding Organisations* (Harmondsworth: Penguin, 1976, 2nd edn 1981), Simon, H. A., *The New Science of Management Decision* (New York: Harper & Row, 1960).

Editors' Bridging Commentary

Chapter 1 drew attention to the various theoretical approaches to the behaviour of the modern large firm. Chapter 2 deals with strategy, the direction in which the firm wishes to move and the logical planning of how objectives are to be achieved.

Strategy implies taking a longer and broader view than the life of the projects being undertaken. It enables the firm to take into account the opportunities and constraints which face the contracting firm, and which are different from those in other sectors because of the low capital base which means that fixed assets are not a constraint in terms of longer term objectives. The diversity of new projects for which the firm may bid also increases the options available to the firm. The relationship between long-term strategic considerations and short term decisions is particularly important in contracting.

2 Business Objectives and Strategy

William Ramsay

'Would you tell me, please, which way I ought to go from here?'
'That depends a good deal on where you want to get to' said the
Cat.
'I don't care where ...' said Alice.
'Then it doesn't matter which way you go' said the Cat.

Lewis Carroll, *Alice's Adventures in Wonderland* (1865)

2.1 MISSION, OBJECTIVES AND STRATEGY

'Strategy' has now become a word in business which is widely used,
and consequently devalued, and is still poorly understood. It is
necessary, therefore, to define strategy as used in business theory
prior to determining those elements which have relevance for large
contractors in the construction industry.

Many firms in the construction industry would probably not see any
need for strategy in their business. In many industries, it is common
for the owner or manager of the firm to say that strategy is unknown
in his business, and then proceed to outline quite clearly what his
business is about and in which direction it is heading: in other words,
he can present a very succinct strategy without realising it. The point
is that a strategy exists for every business, however big or small,
whether such a strategy is implicit or explicit. The latter is preferable,
if only because the key managers in that firm can then understand and
appreciate the context of their activities.

Strategy, tactics and logistics are all business terms which derive
from a military source. Strategy comes from the Greek word for
general: *strategos*. It is defined in the Oxford English Dictionary as
'generalship, the art of war: management of an army or armies in a
campaign, art of so moving or dispersing troops or ships as to *impose
upon your enemy the place and time and conditions for fighting
preferred by oneself*' (my italics). The key lies in the last three words.

9

For the essence of business strategy is to try to arrange things so that you are in control of the situation; ideally, you should break the resistance of competition without a fight. This can be achieved if your competitor really believes that there will be little or no profit in continuing to compete under the existing conditions, as he sees them. Strategy is usually proactive. Many contractors in the construction industry are often simply reactive.

Strategy has to be placed in its proper context for the business firm. Effectively, objectives come before strategy. Strategy is about the means of meeting these objectives which, in turn, are determined by the mission of the business itself. These factors: mission, objectives and strategy are clearly interrelated, and each loops back on the others to form a complete and meaningful entity as shown in Figure 2.1.

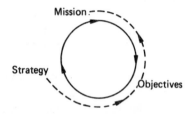

Figure 2.1 Interrelationship of objectives, strategy and mission

The mission (or vision) of a business is its long term ambition, what it *ideally* wants to become over time. This is usually expressed in qualitative terms, and is probably never achieved exactly or totally. Objectives are finite in time, shorter term and mainly quantitative. Some private companies can reduce their objectives to one overriding financial objective. For most public companies, however, objectives are not just financial but also reflect the interest of the various parties or stakeholders involved – e.g., stockholders, employees, customers and the community in which the firm operates. Objectives are set to provide measures of performance, and are effectively attributes over time related to each of these stakeholders: growth in the case of volume and/or revenue, efficiency for absolute profits or the ratio of profits to sales, utilisation of resources for return on investment (ROI) or return on equity (ROE), shareholders' contributions for dividends or earnings per share. Objectives in the form of attributes can also be expressed in terms of price and quality of product relative to competition, employee remuneration and rate of employee turn-over, or even of the firm's contribution to the community. The time frame is important if only as one way to reconcile conflicting objectives. This is variable, usually up to five years.

The management of the firm should be committed to the objectives of the business. There is obviously no point in developing a strategy to meet certain objectives if there is no commitment to them in the first place. Here again comes the interrelationship of mission, objectives and strategy (Figure 2.1). This holds true regardless of size of firm or type of industry.

2.2 THE STRATEGY STATEMENT

Drucker suggests that strategic planning consists of the answers to three questions: what *is* our business? what *will* it be? what *should* it be?[1] These are deceptively simple questions which require consider-able analysis and thought before they can be properly answered. The concentration on defining the business of the firm highlights the need to understand exactly what the firm is about, the boundaries of its business and the need to add to or to subtract from this position in the light of the market environment and of the competitive situation in which the firm finds itself.

The literature on strategy defines it both including and excluding objectives. If objectives are excluded, strategy is 'the fundamental pattern of present and planned resource deployment and environ-mental interactions that indicate how the organisation will achieve its objectives'.[2]

Such a strategy has four distinct components or threads.'[3] The first component is the scope of the business. How is the business defined – i.e., what is its extent and its limits? This should be expressed in functional rather than in physical terms. For example, Levitt[4] has argued that many railway companies were unsuccessful because they concerned themselves with running trains, and did not realise they were effectively in the business of transporting people.

Determination of the scope of the business 'is probably the most important strategic question that general managers confront, since it provides a context within which all other strategic questions can be considered'.[5]

A business may be defined in three ways. First, *who* is being satisfied? This identifies the categories of customer or groups of customers. Second, *what* is being satisfied? It is important to set down the various needs of the customer relative to the function of the business. And third, *how* are these needs being satisfied? Each firm has some expertise or technology which is used in the process of satisfying distinct customer needs.

Most markets serve many different customer groups and a wide range of customer needs, and require different types of marketing approach. Any business firm should understand the available methods of market segmentation and decide on its particular approach – that is, will it attempt to satisfy most segments of the market or will it focus specifically on one or two segments? Positioning is the act of explicitly determining the firm's choices in this respect.

The second component or thread in the strategic statement is the resource deployment or distinctive competences of the business. The allocation of resources – funds, fixed assets and people – in terms of priority is a significant strategic decision. If the firm really believes, for example, that people are its most important attribute and the factor that distinguishes it from its competition, it will act accordingly and spell this out in its strategy. Every firm, like every individual, is skilled in specific areas. These skills should be recognised and confirmed.

The third thread of the strategy is to specify the competitive advantages of the firm. These are not simply a rerun of its distinctive competences, which may equally be characteristics of other competitors. Competitive advantages identify exactly where the firm is superior to its competition. This is not limited to the quality of the end product itself but includes aspects of the total business process where it enjoys an edge over its competitors in packaging, distribution, or purchasing.

The fourth and final thread in the statement of strategy is concerned with synergy. Various parts or processes of the firm can combine together to create something greater than the actual sum of these parts. For example, in some firms technical research and marketing come together to create new products which are able to promote competitive advantages to support the firm's activities.

The resulting strategy statement should describe each of these four 'threads' or components, indicate how they will lead to the achievement of the objectives, describe the nature of the business in functional rather than physical terms, and be as simple and as precise as possible.

That is the theory. It is true to say that few strategy statements, and even fewer 'good' strategy statements, are publicly available. Obviously, there is an element of competitive secrecy surrounding such statements; at the same time, however, there is also the belief, held by many managers, that such a statement imposes limitations on management and particularly on its potential for innovation, creativity and entrepreneurial flair.

It needs to be stressed, however, that the companies generally regarded as the most successful in terms of sales growth, profitability and returns have well defined strategies.[6] Even in the advertising profession, the executive Vice President of a well known New York agency has stressed the freedom which is provided by a well defined strategy as the basis for creative work.[7]

2.3 STEPS IN STRATEGIC MANAGEMENT

The relevant model of strategic management for the individual firm will depend on the size and complexity of the business. The following seven steps are involved:

1. Establishing the basic mission of the business
2. Determining specific objectives
3. Analysing strengths, weaknesses, opportunities and threats (SWOT)
4. Identifying strategic options
5. Deciding on the strategy and plan
6. Implementing the strategic plan
7. Evaluating progress and control

A strategic plan can be as simple or as complicated as the firm wants. As indicated earlier, it may be a sentence or two in the head of the owner, or it may be an elaboration of different continuous inputs across the very large corporation.

In order to provide a better determination of the firm's objectives, and also to make a start on identifying some of the strategic alternatives to achieve them, it is helpful to conduct an internal analysis of the firm's strengths and weaknesses followed by an external analysis of the market environment in which the firm is operating in order to discover the opportunities available and likely threats. This process is often designated by the acronym SWOT (strengths/weaknesses and opportunities/threats). The factors involved and the intensity of the exercise are variable as the following examples show.

STRENGTHS/WEAKNESSES (Internal)		OPPORTUNITIES/THREATS (External)	
Organisation	Structure	*Market*	Size
	Management skills		Growth
	Operating		Profitability
	procedures	*Competition*	Capacity utilisation
Personnel	Attributes		Barriers to entry/exit
	Experience		
	Numbers	*Economic*	Inflation
Marketing	Sales force	*Government*	Government support
	Customer service		Wage levels
	Breadth of line	*Technology*	Maturity
Operations/	Production facilities		Patents
R&D	Production		Complexity
	Level of know-how	*Social*	Unionisation
Finance	Size		Demographic
	Growth		changes
	P/E ratio		Ecological
			movement

The four elements of the SWOT analysis can be plotted on a two-by-two matrix. This provides something approaching a 'strategic ledger', where the firm can assess areas for improvement and investment on the one hand and for disengagement on the other. On the basis of this ledger, allocation of resources may be carried out with changed priorities. The subsequent review can yield an assessment of the probability of reaching the desired objectives and whether they should be adjusted up or down in the light of the SWOT analysis.

There are several concepts and tools used to formulate strategic alternatives. Several of them feature an analysis of the firm's portfolio of different products or businesses.

The concept of the experience curve is based on the correlation between the level of cost per unit sold and the accumulated volume produced. There is a considerable body of empirical evidence to show that, when volume produced is doubled, the cost per unit can be reduced by between 10–30 per cent. This does not happen automatically, but is possible if we take into account the entire spectrum of the firm's activities – i.e., not only manufacturing but also marketing and distribution, for example. The implications of the experience curve are significant. The volume of any product or business is dependent on the growth of the market and its share of that market. The growth–share matrix was developed by the Boston Consulting Group to enable companies to evaluate the various products or business units in their portfolio (Figure 2.2). The vertical matrix is market growth rate with a cut-off point determined by the user to separate high growth from low growth, with an example here of 6 per cent a year. The horizontal matrix is relative market share – i.e., the share of the product compared with the leading competitor in the market. The cut-off point is 1.5 : 1, which means that a product on that line has a 50 per cent higher share than its leading competitor.

Figure 2.2 shows ten different businesses of a company, the size of

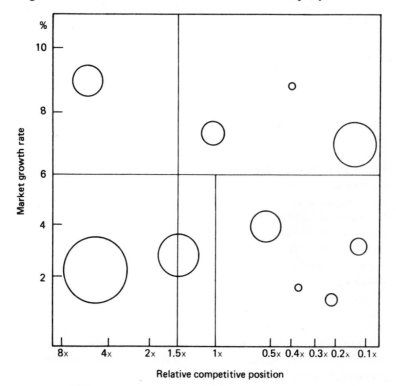

Figure 2.2 Example of growth–share portfolio matrix

Notes: Size of circle indicates sales level. Relative competitive position is measured by ratio of sales of company to that of leading competitor.

Source: Boston Consulting Group, *Perspectives*, Growth–Share Portfolio Mix (1973).

the circles representing the sales revenue of each. Four of the ten are in markets growing faster than 6 per cent but only one business has a clear relative share advantage. Six of the ten units are in markets growing less than 6 per cent and only two of them are clear market leaders.

The implications of each quadrant can be defined for manufacturing industry where investment is necessary to enable growth to take place, though not for contracting (see Section 2.5). The top left quadrant in Figure 2.2 contains high growth, high market share businesses. They are the 'stars' of the portfolio but they probably use as much cash as they generate. The top right quadrant contains high growth businesses which use a lot of cash and, because they are not market leaders, generate little cash – i.e., they are heavy cash users and, therefore, problems. The bottom left quadrant contains the major cash generators of the company: low growth and high share. Such 'cash cows' are used to source the cash users. The bottom right hand quadrant contains the dogs of the company – i.e., low growth, low share businesses which use up whatever cash they generate just to keep going and which eventually have to be divested because they are effectively cash traps. The share–growth matrix is a simple one-shot analysis which can suggest ways of allocating resources within the company. Strategic decisions as to whether to invest, hold, harvest or divest can be suggested for different products or services in the company's portfolio.[8] Its apparent simplicity, however, should not disguise the fact that it is much more complicated than it looks. Just to define the market to which the product or service belongs can be fraught with difficulty. Many market definitions are either too large or too small to be meaningful.

The advantage of the growth–share matrix is its ability to examine the portfolio of the company on two dimensions. The attractiveness of a market or industry, however, lies in more than simply its level of growth. Equally, the strength of a firm in running a specific business lies in more than just market share. This led to the development by General Electric and McKinsey of a business assessment array which examined various factors of industry attractiveness on one side and of business strength on the other. Industry attractiveness might include size, growth, concentration, and profitability. Business strength relative to a specific industry could consist of relative product quality, price competitiveness, technical know-how, selling ability and the calibre of the firm's management. There is some overlap here with the overall SWOT analysis referred to earlier. The assessment of an array of factors specific to the particular businesses of the company again relies a good deal on judgement. In order to provide a form of quantification, each factor can be assigned a numerical rating, and the ratings weighted in order to provide a total weighted score. This may result in too much reliance being placed on numerical evaluation; the objective is to provide an overall high, medium or low assessment for both industry attractiveness and business strengths. The different businesses of the company are plotted on the industry attractiveness–business strength matrix (Figure 2.3).

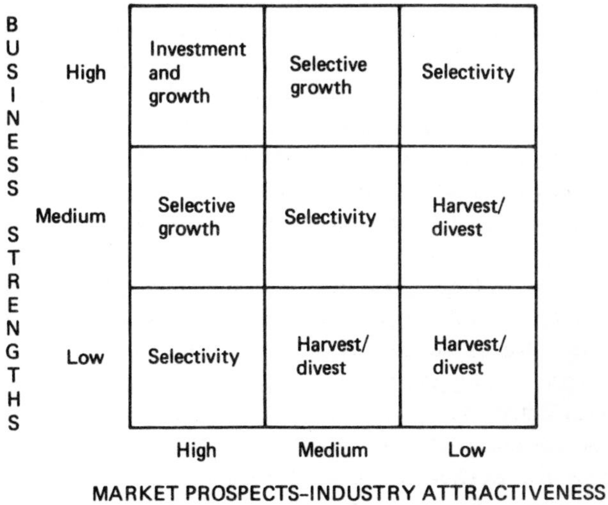

B U S I N E S S S T R E N G T H S		Investment and growth	Selective growth	Selectivity
	High	Investment and growth	Selective growth	Selectivity
	Medium	Selective growth	Selectivity	Harvest/ divest
	Low	Selectivity	Harvest/ divest	Harvest/ divest
		High	Medium	Low

MARKET PROSPECTS–INDUSTRY ATTRACTIVENESS

Figure 2.3 Industry attractiveness and business strengths matrix

Source: General Electric and McKinsey, in Wind, Y. and Mahajan, V., 'Designing Product and Business Portfolios', *Harvard Business Review*, vol. 59, no. 1, (January/February 1981) pp. 155–65.

The purpose of the business assessment array is to assign priorities for the allocation of total company resources. There are four groups of priorities shown in Figure 2.3: investment and growth in the top left box, which is high on both counts; selective growth; selectivity, for either growth or harvesting; and finally the three boxes in the bottom right corner which suggest either harvesting or divesting.

The business array matrix and its variants[9] avoid the simplicity of the growth–share matrix but substitute greater judgement. Both techniques have a role to play. They are particularly useful not just for the firm looking at its own business portfolio but also for the firm analysing its competition and attempting to determine what strategy competitors might be following as a result of judging their business in the same way.

2.4 COMPETITIVE STRATEGY

To confirm the point just made, it is no longer sufficient for the firm to determine its own business strategy. It must also be prepared to work out its strategy in the context of the overall competitive scene, and to determine roughly what strategies its competitors may follow – or at least how such competitors might react to the strategic plans of the firm.

The following section draws on the work of Michael Porter. He is an industrial economist at Harvard who has written two major books: 'Competitive Strategy' and 'Competitive Advantage'.[10] Porter's ongoing premise is that the ultimate profit potential of an industry is a function of its competitive intensity, which in turn is related to the structure of the industry. Industry structure and profitability are determined by five competitive forces – namely entry barriers, pressure from substitute products, the bargaining power of both buyers and suppliers, and the intensity of rivalry among existing competitors. It is not enough simply to look at current competitors. One must also anticipate possible developments from outside the industry. For example, an industry will enjoy high and stable profits when the firms in that industry can deal effectively with the threats posed by new entrants and technical substitutes, neutralise the bargaining power of both suppliers and buyers and, at the same time, maintain a moderate competitive rivalry among themselves.

Each of these five factors should be continually examined to anticipate possible changes which will affect future profitability. A change in one factor strongly influences the others. If the cost of switching to alternate products or services is significantly reduced, the impact is felt across all the competitive forces.

The primary objective of a firm's strategy is to secure a sustainable advantage in the market against its competition. Porter suggests there are three generic strategies to achieve this: (1) to obtain overall cost leadership to obtain industry wide advantage, (2) to differentiate the product for the same purpose, or (3) to focus on a particular market segment using either low cost or differentiation.

Effectively, however, there are only two basic strategies: one based on cost, the other on differentiation. The third is really a variant of the first two. The basis of a cost leadership strategy in an industry is to pursue very aggressively a low cost structure across the firm's entire business system. This will build highly efficient scale facilities, pursue cost reductions based on the experience curve, exercise tight overhead controls, eliminate marginal customer accounts, and minimise costs across all fronts of the business – e.g., R & D, sales and advertising. Companies such as Texas Instruments, Black & Decker and Dupont use this strategy.

The second strategy concentrates on the advantage of differentiation against all other mainstream competitors – that is, it creates something perceived by the customer as unique. This may lie in product design, technology, specific features of the product, customer service or a particular distributive network. It will distinguish the product, brand or service from its competition by means of a specific image. Examples of this strategy are companies such as Sony, BMW and Remington Shaver.

The third strategy (the variant of the other two) focuses on a particular segment of the total market and does not try to compete on an industry-wide basis. The firm's strategy is to serve a narrow strategic target better than competitors who operate more broadly. It can achieve this either by lower costs in serving this market or by differentiation in better meeting the needs of this particular market. People's Express airline in the USA (and Laker unsuccessfully in the UK) and Toyota in the USA exemplify focused cost advantage, while Mercedes Benz and Jaguar in the UK market are examples of focused differentiation.

The decision as to which of the two basic strategies to follow is important. Companies often try to do both and then finish up with neither a cost advantage nor any distinctive values. Equally, all these strategies have risks. Cost leadership can be undermined by technological change, by newcomers to the industry taking advantage of prior experience, and by too much emphasis on cost at the expense of marketing. Differentiation often begets a premium price which may become too large, or the perception of product value may narrow over time. Focus is usually a balance between becoming too large (resulting in further segmentation) and being too small to sustain a large business. The latter fate befell American Motors who created the segment for small cars in the USA only to see the two major manufacturers, GM and Ford, enter this segment as well.

An extremely important thread in the strategy statement is the identification of the firm's competitive advantages.

The business system of McKinsey,[11] as a representation of the sequence of steps by which companies in a given business produce their products or services and get them to their customers, is helpful. As an example, Figure 2.4 illustrates the business system for a typical manufacturing company.

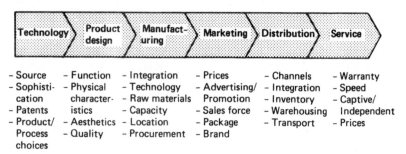

Technology	Product design	Manufact-uring	Marketing	Distribution	Service
– Source	– Function	– Integration	– Prices	– Channels	– Warranty
– Sophisti-cation	– Physical character-istics	– Technology	– Advertising/ Promotion	– Integration	– Speed
– Patents		– Raw materials	– Sales force	– Inventory	– Captive/
– Product/ Process choices	– Aesthetics	– Capacity	– Package	– Warehousing	Independent
	– Quality	– Location	– Brand	– Transport	– Prices
		– Procurement			

Figure 2.4 Business system for a manufacturing company
Source: McKinsey, *New Game Strategies*, Staff Paper (New York, 1980).

This framework can be used in a number of ways. It can provide sources of competitive advantage, either current or potential, such as special features in the product design of calculators. Equally each step can be examined to determine the sources of economic leverage in the system – e.g., product yield in the manufacturing process. Both of the above can be determined not only for the firm itself but also for its competition. In this process, it is possible to detect what are the key factors of success (KFS) in the particular market under examination. This business system approach is similar to the value chain concept of Porter which consists of all the 'value activities' performed by a firm plus its profit margin. These 'value activities' include both primary activities (e.g., line operations) and support activities (e.g., staff overheads). Porter argues that every value activity embodies technology of some kind. In linking them together, value activities become the 'discrete building blocks of competitive advantage'.[12] Value activities are not standard accounting classifications, nor are they simply another way of describing value added. Rather, they are assigned on judgement to different categories that best represent their contribution to a firm's competitive advantage. A firm has to determine the structural factors that influence cost – i.e., 'cost drivers' – and the value activities that can be a potential source of uniqueness – i.e., 'uniqueness drivers'. The key strategic issue is how the firm can achieve an overall sustainable competitive advantage either in terms of cost *or* of uniqueness. Competitive advantage of either kind should consist of several different factors and not be limited to one factor alone. In order to achieve such an overall competitive advantage, it may be necessary to reconfigure the value chain. Understanding what drives the market, and the company itself, is obviously an important breakthrough in strategic analysis. Another breakthrough becomes possible when an attempt is made to change or to reconfigure the business system. The latter has been explored by use of the concept of the strategic gameboard (Figure 2.5). This looks at the scope of competition – i.e., where to compete – on one side and the mode of competition – i.e., how to compete – on the other. [13]

The scope of competition is divided into 'across the board' (industry-wide) and 'selective': focus. The mode of competition is

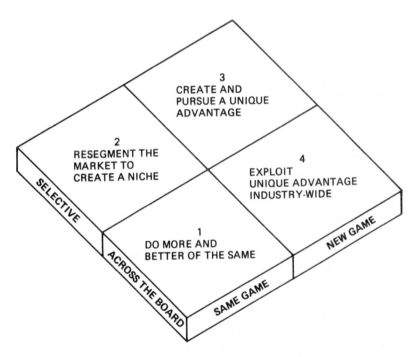

Figure 2.5 The strategic gameboard

Source: McKinsey, *New Game Strategies*, Staff Paper (New York, 1980).

divided into 'same game' or 'new game'. Accordingly, we have four strategic options in the different quadrants. The first option is to play the same game across the board. In order to gain a competitive advantage, the firm has to do more and better. For example, Miller Beer, after its acquisition by Philip Morris, greatly strengthened its marketing activities with a series of new products and increased advertising, which took it from No. 5 brand in the US beer market to No. 2 position. The second option is again to play the same game as competition, but to do so on a selective basis – i.e., create a specific niche in the market. There are several examples of this strategy in the premium-price car market.

Most strategies today are versions of playing the same game. To play a new game is obviously much more risky and involves discarding much conventional thinking about how to compete in any given market. When it works, it can pay off handsomely. The third option involves taking the new game route on an industry-wide basis by exploiting some unique advantage over the competition. This usually involves a major change in the value chain or business system, often in the area of distribution. For example, the success of Timex and Seiko lay in deciding to sell their watches in supermarkets and discount stores rather than limiting themselves to the speciality jewellery stores as traditional Swiss watch producers did. Procter and Gamble's huge success in Pampers lay in their ability to exploit their unique technology in soft paper diapers using their distribution strength in grocery stores. The fourth option also plays a new game but in a specific segment. Laker Airways did not attempt to compete with other airlines across the board but focused on the highly profitable London–New York segment where Skytrain provided a totally new kind of low-cost service: guaranteed ticket at the gate and no frills.

The four options are by no means watertight compartments, and elements of each can often be found in company strategies.

2.5 RELEVANCE OF BUSINESS STRATEGY TO THE LARGE CONTRACTOR

What is the relevance of business strategy to the large contractor in the construction industry? Many contractors would argue that their business is simply about 'getting, doing and getting paid'. Where is the need for high-falutin' theory and intricate analyses in what is essentially a pragmatic, literally down-to-earth business where few facts are readily available? There is some force behind these arguments, particularly for small contractors and subcontractors.

There are two broad aspects of management in the contracting industry. The first is project management, which is concerned with managing people, developing loyalty and team spirit, and with the efficient logistics of individual assignments. The second lies at headquarters, and involves the strategic thinking necessary to achieve a better sense of direction thereby increasing long term financial returns for the total company.

In this latter area, the concepts of business strategy have been developed primarily for manufacturing industry. The process involved in manufactured goods is turned upside down by the contracting industry. In contracting, it has been the client (customer) who initiates the project (product). The contractor (producer) has limited control over the contract (formulation–design). The price is agreed before the project (product) is started.

It is no surprise, therefore, that several aspects of business strategy have little relevance to the contracting industry, although some do have limited applicability. Life cycle theory argues that a product, or even an industry, follows a typical pattern through four different phases: introduction, growth, maturity and decline. Business strategy varies at each stage. The life cycle theory might seem to be irrelevant in contracting though, in fact, it has been used. Just like any brand franchise, the image of an individual contractor needs to be refurbished over time. The findings from PIMS' (Profit Impact of Marketing Strategies)[14] pooled experience have no immediate relevance, but only because specific input from the contracting industry would be required to determine their validity. Game theory[15] has been evaluated by contractors, but this involves both legal and moral issues such as competitors agreeing to influence the level of bidding. The difficulty of applying the experience curve directly lies in determining what is a constant unit of value in contracting (it is not that easy sometimes in manufacturing). Similar types of projects do provide the benefits of experience. For example, the second generation of AGR nuclear power stations benefited from the experience gained in the first set. Such projects can often be few and far between, and each project has its own individual circumstances.

Nevertheless, some aspects of business strategy do have relevance for large-scale contracting. Two clearly discernible trends in the industry are becoming more evident. First, the industry is becoming increasingly concentrated as a result of acquisitions and mergers. Some of these acquisitions have seen extraordinary growth for contracting businesses based on a well conceived strategy. Secondly, many large scale contractors are diversifying away from their original base. In this process, such companies are effectively changing the scope of their business by redefining their competitive position within the industry, and are looking for effective segments or niches within the total market. Much of this diversification is closely associated with contracting – e.g., timber merchanting or plant hire – or is developed from a contracting base – e.g., from building houses to speculative housing development. Some contractors are moving into fields in which some of the skills learned in contracting may be applied – e.g., property investment, opencast coal mining and making building materials. Others have been spreading their business outside the UK, effectively a form of geographic segmentation, capitalising on their know-how and experience. Here it is important to determine who the global competitors are – e.g., Korean companies are new multi-nationals using different techniques in international contracting.

Few of the top 50 largest contractors in the UK are now simply just building and civil engineering contractors.[16] It is important, there-fore, for the contractor to identify clearly what business he is in, the position he occupies in that business, and who are his present and potential competitors – these are all elements of business strategy. In this process of self-definition, he will find that he is in several different businesses or that 'strict contracting' is really part of a broader portfolio. In 1980, two in every five leading contractors were subsidiary companies. Whether he knows it or likes it, the contractor is involved in portfolio management. 80 per cent of the leading contractors have a pre-interest profit to tangible capital employed in double figures, and most of them generate positive cash flow every year. In a diversified management portfolio, therefore, contracting becomes a short term cash generator. Fairly simple analysis would be able to determine whether parts of the large contractor's business are 'stars' or fall into other portfolio categories; this analysis would provide guidelines for investment priority and resource allocation. When deciding where to diversify, an assessment of the attractiveness and drawbacks of the new market and the strengths and weaknesses of the contractor would help to quantify intuitive judgement without necessarily incurring great effort or expenditure. When the market opportunity has been confirmed, the decision on whether to compete on the basis of lower cost or to offer some form of differentiation has to be made. The likely reaction of current competition should also be assessed.

What are the key factors for success in the contracting business? A major issue, if not the central issue, is the *process* of construction. The four phases: conceptual, design, contract documentation and construction on site[17] not only add up to a complex process for the contractor, but also one where his room for manoeuvre is quite limited. A key element in the definition of strategy is the ability of the participant to set down the conditions 'preferred by oneself' (see Section 2.1 above). In the contracting process, specifications and tendering conditions are usually imposed upon the contractor. This means that the only way to influence or to change the conditions is to bid or to act in such a way as virtually to opt out of the process. The peculiarities of the bidding situation in construction make it necessary for the contractor to retain a high degree of flexibility in his positioning.

Several changes are taking place in the construction process. There is an increase in contractor-led design and construct projects and in management contracting, both of which allow the contractor more control; the move towards greater property investment and speculative housing activity by some large contractors also provides greater control. Market segmentation is now becoming more prevalent – geography and size of contract have always been important in this respect. Increasingly, there are more varieties in the type of contract,[18] and in the services provided by the contractor. There is great specialisation by the contractor in the type of work sought. There is segmentation by customers whereby the contractor seeks to establish a special relationship with target clients in growth industries such as retailing. These are all instances where the large contractor is involved in strategic segmentation.

To provide satisfactory answers, the large contractor is faced with basic questions of competitive strategy: first, how attractive is the contracting business and why, and second, what is determining his relative position within contracting? In order to answer the first question, he will review the forces that affect industry profitability (the nature of cyclical demand in construction and its impact on entry and exit from contracting), the bargaining power both of clients who effectively buy his services and of suppliers of raw materials and subcontracting services, the level of repair and maintenance which can be regarded as substitutes for new building or engineering projects, and the structure and level of concentration within contracting and the consequent degree of rivalry within the business.

In order to answer the second question, the contractor has to review the stages, and the activities within each stage, which add up to the total value of the end product he is creating. These stages and activities are not simply accounting classifications. In construction projects, they might consist of: Feasibility – Design – Bidding – Construction – Handover. The actual names of the stages are not important; what is important is that these stages are identified clearly and in sufficient detail to enable the contractor to pinpoint improvements either by further added value (technical or quality upgrading) or by cost reduction which will achieve for his business a number of different advantages over his competitors. This is not an easy task, and requires a relatively high degree of creativity in reorganising, changing or eliminating certain activities within the total process.

It is probable that the above kind of analysis and its resolution are more difficult in the contracting industry than in most other industries where the same product is produced in roughly the same way in large quantities. The difficulty of achieving a realistic cost estimate in strictly accounting terms is well known. To assess the total value of contracting projects in non-accounting terms is even more tenuous. This is because a service industry deals much more with intangibles than a manufacturing business.

Nevertheless, change comes only when you try. The nature of the contracting process has remained unchanged for a long time, and tradition has played its familiar role. Every examination, analysis and commission on the construction industry has arrived at similar conclusions – they have deplored the slow rate of change, the low level of R & D, the innate conservatism and the lack of innovation within the industry. They have emphasised the need for solutions which look at the total entity of the industry, not at piecemeal revisions.

Change is now on the way. There is the need for a bold strategy which clearly understands the current rules of the game and is prepared to change them, to reconfigure the existing process and to play a new game.

Who should be the agent for change in this strategy? It is not likely to be the client, who is often quite unsophisticated and plays no role in actually creating the end product. It is not likely to be the professional architect or engineer, since change militates against his own economic interest and his present position of privilege. The agent for change must be the contractor, for he is the only party who is able to take the process apart and put it together again, thereby creating a new kind of market which provides even better and longer lasting value to the client. This will yield a business strategy which he can effectively control. In the long run, it will be in the interest of society which will benefit from a more truly competitive market.

2.6 CONCLUDING REMARKS

As volume is depressed, the development of business strategy accelerates – or, to put it another way, strategy seems less necessary when things are going well. Once again, construction may be the exception. Despite cyclical depressions, and volume declines, business strategy has had little ostensible impact on the construction industry. It is an industry which is different from others for all the reasons usually quoted: the physical nature of the product, the complex structure of the industry, the length of the construction process.

Every practice rests on theory, even if the practitioners themselves are unaware of it.[19] Drucker is speaking of entrepreneurship; every businessman – and here the contractor is no exception – likes to think of himself as an entrepreneur. The contractor, as entrepreneur, should explore the theory that lies behind his business.

This theory to date has been dominated by economics. It has been suggested[20] that biology may be more relevant than economics in the development of a useful competitive theory. This starts from Darwin's conclusions that the struggle for survival is more severe among species with the same characteristics than among those with different characteristics: 'No two competitors can co-exist who make their living in the same way. Their relationship is unstable. One will displace the other'.[21] Each business firm, in order to survive, must determine the boundaries of its particular position so that it does not compete on identical terms. In this respect, contracting is not an exception. Each contractor must determine the skills he has to offer, and what sustainable advantages he can create *vis-à-vis* his competition. Theory is easy to write, much more difficult to put into practice. In strategy, there is often a wide gap between planning and implementation: 'The best plan is only a plan unless it degenerates into work'.[22]

There are difficulties inherent in strategic planning for the contracting industry that are both long standing and prevalent across many countries, not merely the UK. Strategic answers will be neither easy nor immediate. The successful contractor in developing a business strategy will not readily accept the status quo. He will recognise that he is in a position to bring about change in the construction process, change which will result in what Schumpeter called 'creative destruction'. In the process, however, the contractor will forge a new market and a new kind of customer.

NOTES AND REFERENCES

1. Drucker, P. F., *Management: Tasks, Responsibilities, Practices* (New York: Harper & Row, 1973) p. 122.
2. Hofer, C. W. and Schendel, D., *Strategy Formation: Analytical Concepts* (St Paul, Minn.: West, 1978) p. 25.
3. Ansoff, H. I., *Corporate Strategy: An Analytical Approach to Business Policy for Growth and Expansion* (New York: McGraw-Hill, 1965).
4. Levitt, T., 'Marketing Myopia', *Harvard Business Review*, Vol. 38, No. 4 (July–August 1960).
5. Abell, D. F., *Defining the Business* (New York: Prentice-Hall, 1980) p. 217.
6. Harvey, D. F. *Business Policy and Strategic Management* (Columbus, Oh.: Merrill, 1983); pp. 21–2 list eight different studies which support the favourable results of strategic planning.
7. Norman Berry, of Ogilvy & Mather Inc., New York, in 'Viewpoint', their House Magazine.
8. See Barry, H. 'Strategy and the Business Portfolio', *Long Range Planning*, Vol. 10, No. 1 (February 1977) pp. 9–15 for more detail on the growth–share matrix.
9. See Wind, Y. and Mahajan, V., 'Designing Product and Business Portfolios', *Harvard Business Review*, Vol. 59, No. 1 (January–February 1981) pp. 155–65. This lists several other variants of the business array technique, such as the directional policy matrix adopted by Royal Dutch Shell.
10. Porter, M. E., *Competitive Strategy – Techniques for Analysing Industries and Competitors* (New York: Free Press, 1980) and *Competitive advantage – Creating and Sustaining Superior Performance* (New York: Free Press, 1985).
11. McKinsey, *New Game Strategies*, a McKinsey Staff Paper (New York, 1980). This section leans heavily on this paper.
12. Porter (1985) (see note 10) p. 38.
13. The concept of the strategic gameboard is developed in McKinsey (1980) (see note 11).
14. PIMs (Profit Impact of Marketing Strategies) uses empirical evidence from a cross-section of different businesses to identify the factors that are correlated with ROI and cash flow. It is operated by the Strategic Planning Institute, Boston and London.

15. Game theory provides a conceptual framework for making decisions applicable not only to games such as poker but to bidding situations. The standard reference is Neumann J. von and Morgenstern, O., *Theory of Games and Economic Behaviour* (Princeton, N. J.: Princeton University Press, 1944).

16. See the *Jordan Survey of British Construction Companies* (1980) carried out on 162 of the largest contractors with detail on the top 50.

17. Hillebrandt, P. M., *Analysis of the British Construction Industry* (London: Macmillan, 1984).

18. The British Property Federation has drawn up different forms of contract.

19. Drucker, P. F., *Innovation and Entrepreneurship: Practice and Principles* (London: Heinemann, 1985) p. 23.

20. Henderson, B., *The Logic of Business Strategy* (Cambridge, Mass.: Ballinger, 1984) pp. 15–25.

21. Henderson (1984) (see note 20) p. 20. This is Gause's Law of Mutual Exclusion.

22. Drucker (1973) (see note 1).

Editors' Bridging Commentary

Diversification is one of the strategic options available to the contracting company and diversification policy is part of strategy, as outlined in Chapter 2.

In its broadest sense, diversification means the expansion of a firm in the direction either of its suppliers and customers (vertical integration), or of different activities (horizontal diversification). Diversification is therefore strongly related to the growth strategy of the firm.

The theory of diversification has focused on the manufacturing firm, and not all the features of the theory can be applied to contracting. The elements which are most relevant to contracting are those which deal with the need to spread risk and to overcome fluctuations in workload and with the decline in the markets of the firm. Also relevant to contracting is the proposition that diversification offers an opportunity for more efficient use of available resources, notably skilled personnel and cash.

Chapter 3 discusses the main aspects of the theory and the relative merits of diversification both by internal expansion and by merger or takeover.

The last section considers the attractiveness of the ownership of contracting companies by conglomerates or by large firms in other industries, and the advantages and disadvantages that accrue to both parties.

3 Diversification

Jacqueline Cannon and
Patricia M. Hillebrandt

3.1 INTRODUCTION

In this chapter, 'diversification' is defined as the process by which
firms extend the range of their business operations outside those in
which they are currently engaged. This broad definition includes (a)
the process referred to as backward vertical integration – that is, the
acquisition or development of businesses whose products are inputs
to the firm's own main operations, (b) forward integration – that is,
the extension of the firm's activities to those of the normal purchaser
of its products, (c) horizontal diversification – that is, a movement
into other markets not involving the firm in any vertical relationships
as in (a) and (b) above. Any of these forms of expansion may take
place either by internal development or by merger or takeover.

3.2 THEORIES OF DIVERSIFICATION

3.2.1 Introduction

A number of theories have been developed to explain the reasons for
diversification. The reasons for diversification may be linked back to
the objectives of the firm, which may be, or include, increases in
profits, rate of profit, value of assets and turnover. Growth in some
form or other is usually the driving force for diversification: 'Marris
recognised that firms are usually multi-product and that diversification into new products is not just an important vehicle of competition
but the major engine of corporate growth.'[1] Growth may be the
result of either positive strategic decisions of the firm or of defensive
decisions, and all diversification moves by the firm involve risk and
uncertainty. The choice of the direction of diversification will be
influenced not only by growth motives but also by the opportunity to
eliminate some undesirable features in the operation of the firm, or to
acquire some special advantages.

If the firm is aiming at growth then it may consider what is the most

31

beneficial method in relation to the opportunities available externally and to its own resources. It may decide to grow by developing its own internal resources, especially if it has excess capacity, or to purchase or merge with another company. The difficulties in growing internally are (1) the possible lack of resources and particularly know-how, (2) the cost of purchasing these resources, especially in a time of expansion in the market, and (3) the time taken to develop the new product and build up the new facility – for example, the long process of construction of new buildings, including the pre-construction phase, the delivery time for plant and machinery and the time required to recruit and train skilled personnel. A great advantage of internal growth is that the new and existing parts of the enterprise are totally integrated. Another benefit is that the new venture can be organised and managed in sympathy with the characteristics of the firm, and mistakes can be rectified at each stage. There is no lack of information on a new internal development but it is very difficult and costly to obtain all relevant commercial data on another company. In theoretical terms there are high transaction costs in obtaining the maximum amount of information about a company and in purchasing it. If savings are made in transaction costs – that is, in obtaining all the information which is really required – the risks of an unsuitable purchase are even greater.

One of the reasons for wanting to expand outside the existing business of the company is that there are barriers to growth in existing products. Those barriers may be related to a market which is declining or not capable of further expansion, to one in which the particular firm has a monopoly position which inhibits further growth, or to one with a few producers where upsetting the equilibrium by increasing market share could be costly. The barriers to growth may also be related to the power of a supplier or to a long term supply shortage.

3.2.2 Vertical integration

Davies[2] in a review of vertical integration[3] distinguishes three main strands of theories which seek to explain the reasons for vertical integration.

The market failure approach

Following the work by Coase and Williamson,[4] it is argued that wherever the costs of relying on the market and undertaking transactions through the market are greater than the costs of in-house production, firms may wish to diversify into the business of their suppliers and/or into the business of their customers. According to Williamson, vertical integration is more likely when there is a high degree of uncertainty in the firm's environment and when transactions recur frequently so that transaction costs would be high.

Technological interdependence

Technological interdependence is usually referred to in terms of economies in the steel industry, but Davies suggests that there are many other different instances of technological interdependence of a type referred to as 'site specific'. This is a case where durable assets are immobile and transacting problems are dealt with through common ownership.

Monopolistic motives for integration

There are a number of different ways in which a monopoly firm can combine with another firm which may itself be a monopolist or operating in a competitive situation. There is not complete agreement amongst theorists as to the potential gains from mergers.

The reduction of uncertainty is a higher motive for vertical integration. Backward vertical integration is justified by the need to overcome a failure of existing suppliers to meet the firm's demand at the time required, in the right quantity, at the right quality, and at a reasonable price. It also enables the firm to increase its market power, either by increasing existing barriers to entry or by creating new ones. An uncertainty concerns the future level of input prices, where downstream firms have only restricted data on the prices of inputs and their ability to make efficient decisions is adversely affected. A third case is that where there is uncertain demand for the product of the downstream industry, though integration may not necessarily be the correct solution to this problem.

3.2.3 Horizontal diversification

Horizontal diversification includes the following categories of association between firms:

1. Diversification by merger with another firm in the same market, sometimes known as horizontal integration. In some countries,

this type of diversification is controlled by monopoly and merger legislation which may well have restricted the number of mergers or takeovers.

2. Diversification into a market which is related to the existing business of the firm, either because of common types of outlets or because of common resources, often implying some synergy between the businesses.

3. Diversification into a market which has no connection with the existing businesses of the firm. This is typical of conglomerate diversification.

This chapter concentrates on types 2 and 3.

An important reason for horizontal diversification is to avoid risk, for example, of fluctuation in the level of demand. The portfolio theory of diversification[5] suggests that horizontal diversification is undertaken to increase the stability of profits by spreading risks or reducing the proportion of high risk businesses in the 'portfolio' of the company. Other reasons to diversify horizontally are to compensate for barriers to expansion in existing markets and to take advantage of the outcome of an unexpected event or of slack in resources, especially highly efficient resources such as outstanding expertise.

Ansoff[6] stresses the importance of synergy in the analysis of mergers. He identifies four types of synergy: sales, operations, investment and management. Synergy derives from commonality of a number of functions relevant both to the existing firm and to the proposed acquisition – for instance, sales synergy is produced by common distribution channels, sales administration, advertising and promotion and reputation. Some of the synergistic effects operate on the demand side – for example, advertising and promotion as well as reputation lead to an increase in the level of demand – whereas common distribution and sales administration lead to a reduction in the level of costs.[7]

Kay regards synergy coupled with the threat of environmental change, notably a fall for external reasons in the demand for the firm's product, as the key to understanding the functioning of the modern highly integrated firm.[8] The demand may fall because of technological change – the development of electricity killed the market for gas lamps – because of increased knowledge, fashion or public opinion, as in the case of the market for cigarettes.

If the market for one product is adversely affected and this product has synergy with another, even though it is not in the same market, the latter will also be adversely affected hence the concept of 'catastrophe linking' introduced by Kay.[9] Diversification which benefits from synergy increases the risk to the overall business because both products are likely to suffer at the same time. Diversification to avoid risk, as in the portfolio theory, thus cannot by definition have the benefit of synergy.

Conglomerates are large multi-product organisations producing goods and services unrelated or only slightly related to each other. Horizontal diversification by conglomerate is a form of cross entry, whereby a firm established in one or several industries takes over or merges with another firm established in an unrelated industry. Conglomerate diversification therefore does not imply increased market power of the same type, as does vertical integration.

The theory relating to conglomerates is reviewed by Clarke.[10] He divides the reasons for the growth of conglomerate firms into two groups: those based on the economies in transaction costs and those relating to financial and managerial factors. Because products of conglomerates are more or less separate, theories of vertical integration do not apply. Economies in transaction costs arise from either:

1. the special advantages in allocating capital to high value uses compared to the normal capital allocation process, or
2. the ability of the conglomerate to make better use of their specialised human and non-human resources by conglomerate growth rather than by selling or leasing their services on the market; in these cases transaction cost advantages arise in markets for resources.[11]

The financial reasons for conglomerate diversification focus essentially on risk reduction. The typical feature of a conglomerate is that it is made up of a mix of businesses, and therefore should be able to avoid excessive variations in performance because poor results in one part of the group are likely to be offset by better results elsewhere. According to the theory, shareholders may not appreciate this advantage as they are able to select their portfolio from a number of industries. However, there are costs of purchase and sale of shares in companies which are related more to the number of transactions than to their value.

Another financial advantage is that conglomerates, by virtue of their size, are able to raise finance more easily and more cheaply than smaller firms. A study by Prais[12] found that the cost of capital to large firms was one or two percentage points lower than for smaller firms, defined as being one-tenth of the size of the large ones.

Finally managerial factors concern the inability of managers in conglomerates to spread their risks in the way shareholders can. Their interest lies in reducing risks of unemployment if the firm performs badly and in increasing the size of the organisation. The way to achieve these two objectives is by adopting a diversification strategy.

3.3 DIVERSIFICATION AND THE CONSTRUCTION FIRM

There are two aspects of diversification to be considered in relation to the contracting firm. The first is where the contracting firm initiates the process and the second is where the diversification process is initiated by a firm outside the industry.

3.1 Diversification by contracting companies

Contracting companies may diversify into a different market in contracting, or into a different industry altogether. There is a problem of definition of a market in construction. At the extreme each project may be considered as a different market because each project takes place in a different geographical area, with a different customer, and often involves a different method of selling. Here a construction market for the firm is defined as that in which a new type of organisation is required to produce in a new location, for a new customer or for a different type of product. The potential reasons for diversification are those described in Section 3.2 above, but not all are of great relevance to construction.

Of the justifications for vertical integration put forward in Section 3.2, market failure and reduction in uncertainty are most relevant to construction. There are several examples of backward integration with contractors moving into the production of building materials to ensure supply, both in quality and timely availability, or to meet unique temporary demand requirements. Contractors have also purchased plant-hire firms and specialist subcontractors for similar reasons and to reduce transaction costs. It is interesting that the whole range of subcontracting, including labour-only subcontracting, can be regarded as the opposite of vertical integration since contractors choose to purchase the services of labour rather than have them internal to the organisation (see Chapter 8).

Since the product of the contracting industry is sold to the final owner, forward integration implies taking on its ownership, and in that way the contractor acts as his own client. His reason for doing so is to create work, to obtain higher profits than are available through contracting work, or to use cash generated by contracting activities (see Chapter 5). Forward integration in manufacturing industry means that the producer goes into the business of his own market to create a demand (such as by becoming a retailer), but he does not become his own final customer. Figures 3.1 a, b, and c below compare traditional contracting with two types of vertical forward integration.

In the traditional contracting model (Fig. 3.1a) the client procures both land and the necessary finance and places an order with the contracting firm. The latter assembles the required resources, manages the production of the building/structure and delivers it to the client. The other two flow charts illustrate situations where the contracting firm acts as developer (3.1b) and as housebuilder (3.1c). In Figure 3.1b, the contracting firm first has to obtain the necessary land and the finance for the project. In effect, it becomes its own client (forward integration) and takes possession of the building/ structure on completion. It may decide to retain its ownership and to use it for its own purposes, to lease it to another organisation, or to sell it.

The difference between the model of the contracting firm as developer (Figure 3.1b) and as housebuilder (Figure 3.1c) is that in the latter case the land and the finance are part of its in-house resources and are shown with its other resources. In addition it can fit its housebuilding programme to the rate of sales and will wish to dispose of its stock to maximise cash flow profit. The developer, by contrast, first has to acquire land and obtain the finance for the project. He can normally dispose of his development as a whole only on final completion. His cash flow is therefore more lumpy.

In construction, two factors are of special importance in explaining horizontal diversification. First there is the secular decline in parts of the market. This has affected, for example, the UK civil engineering industry – and, indeed, that of many other western countries. This may be likened to the catastrophe scenario suggested by Kay (see Section 3.2.3). It is the inevitable consequence of a market where products have very long lives and hence very long replacement

38

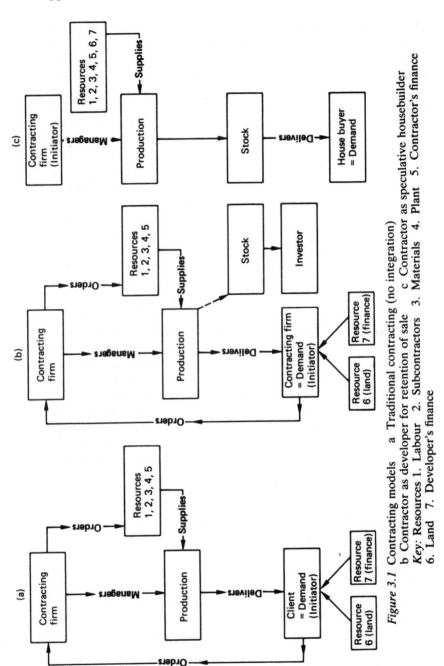

Figure 3.1 Contracting models   a Traditional contracting (no integration)
b Contractor as developer for retention of sale   c Contractor as speculative housebuilder
Key: Resources 1. Labour 2. Subcontractors 3. Materials 4. Plant 5. Contractor's finance
6. Land 7. Developer's finance

waves. Some civil engineering firms have sought to overcome the problem of secular decline by diversifying into the housebuilding industry. A similar incentive to diversify may arise when the market has remained constant but the number or capacity of existing firms far exceeds demand. In both cases, there may well be opportunities for greater profits in new markets.

Secondly, horizontal diversification may be induced by a need for contracting companies to spread risks, and especially to reduce fluctuations in their output, which may be either seasonal or cyclical. Ideally, diversification ought to be into products or geographical markets with a pattern of demand counter-cyclical to that in which the contracting companies are already operating. This is difficult to achieve, and an alternative is to diversify into a market where demand is relatively stable. Because of the importance of fluctuations the risk spreading diversification of portfolio theory is particularly important and many large contractors are in businesses quite different from contracting and often with only tenuous connections with contracting or even construction, so that the synergy is slight.

However, when contractors diversify from one market to another within contracting or from contracting to construction-related markets, synergy may be very strong, particularly in operating and management. Operating synergy includes that derived from common facilities, personnel, overheads, learning curves or inputs. Management synergy refers to the transfer of management experience and skills across businesses. Because the level of fixed assets in the industry is generally low, investment synergy is on the whole weaker than in manufacturing. There is some synergy in sales, particularly because of the importance of reputation of contractors in obtaining work.

A third reason for diversification also applies to construction. The contracting firm may have some excess capacity in its resources, such as in management, plant, cash or in a particular expertise, which it can utilise either in horizontal or in vertical integration.

3.3.2 Diversification into contracting

Where diversification is initiated by a firm outside the industry, the first reason for diversifying specifically into contracting is to increase the return on capital employed (ROCE), since contracting firms have low capital requirements and high cash flow. The second is to improve the viability of other subsidiary companies especially those which are cash-hungry or are suppliers to, or customers of, contracting firms.

The contracting firm taken over or merged with a manufacturing firm or a conglomerate derives some advantages from being part of this organisation:

1. The firm acquires greater stability through its ownership by a larger organisation and close relationships with fellow subsidiaries.
2. Stability is further enhanced since the contracting company's fluctuations/cycles are different from those of the other activities of the group.
3. Obtaining work may be facilitated by the reputation of the parent company, especially abroad.
4. The financial strength of the group gives the contracting subsidiary an edge over other competitors.
5. The company may have access to a wider range of fringe benefits to retain and attract skilled personnel.
6. The company may be able to exert more pressure politically.
7. The company does not have to try and maintain stable levels of performance for the benefit of the stock exchange.

The main disadvantages of being part of a group or conglomerate are that the company may be set financial targets which may be more suited to the group or to its other subsidiaries than to the contracting company. The activities of the contracting company may be restricted, especially if the group already has subsidiaries operating in related activities such as housebuilding and property development, which would otherwise enable the contracting subsidiary to broaden its profit base. Section 3.2 suggested that contractors had important reasons for deciding to diversify both vertically and horizontally. This broader spread of activity should be beneficial to the industry as a whole if it leads to a more efficient use of resources.

The companion volume, *The Modern Construction Firm*, confirms that the large UK contractors have been diversifying to a substantial extent, especially in the last decade or so. This strategy has had a profound impact on the structure of the industry. Whilst some companies have deliberately gone outside construction-related activities, diversification has on the whole been into areas with which they were already familiar, such as development or building products manufacturing.

Contractors have always maintained that contracting is so different from other processes that it is not possible successfully to transfer a senior manager from manufacturing to contracting. If this is true, whether or not diversification by contracting firms succeeds depends on the ability of their own management to adapt their skills to those required in other industries. It is noteworthy that even in diversified contracting companies, the background of top management is strongly linked to contracting.

In the case of conglomerates, the group's top management tends to be more broadly based, but they leave the management of their contracting subsidiaries in the hands of those with specialist knowledge of the industry. The main concern of the conglomerate's board is financial and for most holdings it will aim at maximising the use and growth of assets. Indeed one of the major reasons for acquiring companies is that conglomerates can make better use of their assets, often within a short time scale. In the case of non-diversified contracting companies, fixed assets will be low and they will be a minor item on the boards' agendas. The main reason for diversifying into contracting is therefore not related to the ability to make better use of their existing assets but to develop the longer term advantages linked to the positive cash flow which contracting activities generate.

Diversification, whether by contracting firms or conglomerates plays an important role in the strategies of those firms and the rate of change in the structure of the contracting industry seems to be accelerating. Whether this will be to the longer term benefit of the industry itself, its clients, suppliers and the professions is not known. There is a need for close investigation of the pace of diversification in the industry, of its evolution, of its impact on the behaviour and performance of diversified contracting firms and of the extent of, and further scope for, diversifying moves.

The major difficulty in establishing such a study lies in the dearth of data on diversification in the construction industry. Indeed, with the growth of conglomerates, published company data on its separate activities are becoming scarcer. This is also true of data on the various operations of diversified contracting companies. Closer relations between research groups and companies should yield the necessary knowledge and understanding.

NOTES AND REFERENCES

1. Quoted in Hay, D. A. and Morris, D. J., *Industrial Economics: Theory and Evidence* (Oxford: Oxford University Press, 1979) p. 280.
2. Davies, S., 'Vertical Integration', in Clarke, R. and McGuinness, T., *The Economics of the Firm* (Oxford: Basil Blackwell, 1987) pp. 83–106.
3. See also Casson, M. C., 'The Theory of Vertical Integration; a Survey and Synthesis', *Journal of Economic Studies*, Vol. 11, No. 2 (1984) pp. 3–43.
4. Coase, R. M., 'The Nature of the Firm', *Economica*, No. 4 (1937) pp. 386–405, reprinted in Stigler G. J. and Boulding, K. E., *Readings in Price Theory* (Homewood, Ill: Irwin, 1952) and Williamson – see, for example, Williamson, O. E., 'The Vertical Integration of Production: Market Failure Considerations', *American Economic Review* Vol. 61 (May 1971) pp. 112–23; Williamson, O. E., 'Transaction Cost Economics: The Governance of Contractual Relations', *Journal of Law and Economics*, Vol. 22 (1979) pp. 233–61.
5. Portfolio theory was originally developed for financial holdings, but is now applied also to the range of businesses of a firm, see Markowitz, H., *Portfolio Selection – Efficient Diversification of Investment* (New York: Wiley, 1959).
6. Ansoff, H. I., *Corporate Strategy* (London: Penguin, 1985) pp. 75–6.
7. Kay, Neil M., *The Evolving Firm: Strategy and Structure in Industrial Organisation* (London: Macmillan, 1982) p. 43.
8. Kay (1982) (see note 7).
9. Kay (1982) (see note 7) p. 75.
10. Clarke, E., 'Conglomerate Firms', in Clarke, E. and McGuinness, T., *The Economics of the Firm* (Oxford: Basil Blackwell, 1987) pp. 107–32.
11. Williamson, O. E., *Markets and Hierarchies: Analysis and Antitrust Implications* (New York: Free Press, 1975), and Williamson, O. E., 'The Modern Corporation: Origins, Evolution, Attributes', *Journal of Economic Literature*, Vol. 19 (1981) pp. 153–68, reported in Clarke (1987) (see note 10).
12. Prais, S. J., *The Evolution of Giant Firms in Britain* (Cambridge: Cambridge University Press, 1976).

Editors' Bridging Commentary

International contracting is a broad market in which to operate, and hence Chapter 4 follows on logically from the chapters on business strategy and diversification. It is a complex area of operations, and the relevant chapter in the companion volume brings out the recent changes which have been taking place in the international market and the responses made by contractors to changing circumstances.

Chapter 4 highlights three necessary conditions for international operations.

1. First the firm should possess some competitive or ownership advantages over firms of the host country and other international companies. In other words, it has to have something special or different to offer.
2. Secondly, these advantages must require exploitation by the enterprise itself, producing in the host country, rather than by selling or licensing these advantages to other firms. Since the contracting firm sells mainly management expertise, when working abroad that should always be provided from within its own organisation.
3. Thirdly, it must be more advantageous for the firm to exploit its advantages by undertaking production outside national borders than to produce domestically and export. In contracting, where the product is immobile and required in a specific location, the decision on where to produce is not determined by the contractor.

4 International Contracting*

Howard Seymour

4.1 INTRODUCTION

The primary objective of this chapter is to integrate those aspects of international construction, some of which have already been mentioned, within a framework of international production economics. The theory of foreign direct investment (FDI) is arguably the most useful tool for this purpose. It allows detailed economic analysis of the firm in an international competitive context and includes the influence both of the country of origin of the enterprise (the 'home country') and the country in which the enterprise is located (the 'host country'). The analysis is founded upon the eclectic paradigm put forward by Dunning.[1] This is an approach which selects the relevant parts of various economic theories and adapts them to analyse and explain the behaviour of international production units, notably the multinational corporation. The framework provides a synthesis of existing theories of FDI and it is a particularly useful vehicle for the industry-specific investigation of international competition in both a micro and macro context. This chapter presents a summary of the eclectic approach, together with the application of the theory to international contracting in Section 4.2. Some policy implications are given in Section 4.3.

4.2 INTERNATIONAL PRODUCTION IN THE CONSTRUCTION INDUSTRY

The theory of international investment in production facilities should not be confused with portfolio investment. FDI is used to set up a production base outside the national borders of the investor country as a means of undertaking international production. As such the investment is intended to maintain control of resources and production facilities. This is clearly not the case in portfolio investment, where the aim is to earn dividends in return for an initial investment

over which the investor relinquishes direct control once the investment is made. FDI and portfolio investment may therefore be
distinguished by the fact that the portfolio investors' decision depends largely on international interest rates, whereas with FDI these
will be only one of a number of determining variables.

Dunning suggests that a firm will undertake international production
provided that three factors are present in any industry; ownership,
internalisation, and locational advantages. While these advantages
are generally analysed in the context of manufacturing activity, they
can equally be expected to arise in the international construction
industry.

It should be noted that in practice the three conditions of the
Dunning framework are likely to be intimately related and therefore
not easily separated in empirical studies. This interaction may be
considered a reflection of the complex nature of international production rather than a weakness of the theoretical framework.

4.2.1 Ownership advantages

The first necessary condition of the Dunning model refers to the
nature of competition within international production:

> *The firm possesses competitive or ownership advantages over firms
> indigenous to the host country, and also over firms of other
> nationalities.*

This condition was first formulated by Hymer[2] and is based upon
industrial organisation theory. Hymer suggested that for enterprises
of one nationality to be involved directly in an industry in another
country, they must acquire or possess assets not available to indigen-
ous firms, or firms of other nationalities that are sufficient to
overcome the disadvantages the enterprise will face in operating in a
new and foreign environment.

The possession or generation of ownership advantages, which
ultimately shape the individual product of the enterprise, can be
derived from three sources: firm-specific, industry-specific, and
country-specific factors. Given that this chapter deals with an
industry-specific situation, that of international contracting, the
emphasis here is on firm-specific and country-specific factors that lead
to the generation of ownership advantages.

Briefly, firm-specific factors are those generated by the firm in order to differentiate its product from those of other firms in the industry. By contrast, country-specific factors are characteristics of the home or host country that the firm may exploit to differentiate itself from enterprises of other nationalities; as such they influence the precise nature of ownership advantages, and are the source of competition that distinguishes international construction from domestic construction. An obvious reason why country-specific factors influence ownership advantages is that countries are not homogeneous in their resources, so that firms originating in different countries are likely to possess different ownership advantages.

Ownership advantages in international contracting are likely to be influenced by the predominant bidding system in the industry. The large number of firms competing for projects in the international market and the nature of the bidding system suggests that firms will aim to differentiate the services they offer to make their initial bids more attractive to the prospective client. The chapter by Ramsay in this volume (Chapter 2) suggests that the strategy of the contractor in a bid may take two potentially related forms: a low cost type strategy where the contractor competes solely upon price, or a differentiation strategy where the contractor aims to differentiate his product from that offered by competitors by various marketing devices. In practice both may be undertaken since they are not mutually exclusive. The interaction of firm-specific and country-specific advantages provides the potential for a strategy such as outlined by Ramsay, while comparative advantage is a source of cost and marketing differentiation. It is therefore useful to summarise the major factors that influence competition within international construction in the context of firm-specific and country-specific factors.

Firm-specific factors

Because the firm must ultimately compete on price and/or product differentiation by the very nature of the bidding system, the major firm-specific ownership advantages are likely to come under three headings:

1. *Name of the firm* The contracting firm's name represents and embodies its past experience, reputation, and specialist expertise. As such, it will be a major source of firm-specific differentiation because it enables the contractor to compete effectively against all others in the industry by the differentiation of the firm in the bid situation.

2. *Human Capital*   The name of the firm reflects the expertise of the firm's workforce. Since the name embodies both the reputation and specialist skills of the contractor, human capital in the form of a skilled and experienced workforce is a major firm-specific ownership advantage to the contractor that ensures product differentiation and additionally affects the rate of tendering success.
3. *Size of the firm*   Generally the larger the enterprise, the more access will it have to cheap finance (via either the loan market or internal funding) and better production resources. This not only enables the contractor to bid for larger contracts, but also gives him the means to acquire a competent workforce, and to diversify into technical and construction-related services that will enable the contractor further to differentiate his product. As these factors may also enhance the reputation of the firm, the size of the contracting company is likely to provide a significant firm-specific advantage.

Country-specific factors

Country-specific factors that influence competition within international construction are likely to come under two general headings – comparative advantage and home country government support:

1. *Comparative advantage*   Porter[3] argues that the notion of comparative advantage suggests that a country will produce goods and services that reflect its relative abundance of capital and labour. A capital-abundant country will thus produce capital intensive goods and services while a labour-abundant country will produce labour-intensive goods and services. Since the major resource of international construction is human capital, comparative advantage within the industry is likely to be reflected in the nature and skills of contractors according to nationality. In the case of South Korea, for example, ready access to a pool of cheap semi-skilled and skilled labour has given its contractors an exploitable ownership advantage that is not available to developed country contractors; the Koreans are well known for their policy of exporting all personnel necessary for construction (including labourers) from the home country to take advantage of their relatively low wage rates and so undercut developed countries' construction costs in overseas markets. At the other end of the scale US contractors have a comparative advantage in the power and process plant construction industry because the construction of, for example,

power, chemical (and particularly petrochemical) plant, is highly dependent on high technology.

Comparative advantage may thus be significant in the general level of expertise offered by contractors of a specific nationality, and as such may provide a major firm-specific advantage for those contractors.

2. *Home country government support* Home government help takes several forms that ultimately rely upon the attitude of that government towards intervention. The French, for example, are renowned for the coordination that the government provides between related sectors of industry, so that French goods and services competing abroad have been likened to a quasi-nationalised industry. In the Korean case, the fact that the government allows only certain contractors to bid abroad and gives them access to home country cheap skilled labour through the Korean armed forces (Korean nationals may be discharged from national service early where their skills are required for overseas construction) provides the Korean contractor with a country-specific advantage not available to other nationality contractors.

Government support has become particularly relevant to competition in international construction in the provision of subsidised export credit for overseas projects. In recent years the decline in the amount of finance for development has led to the situation in many developing regions where the client's top priority in the bidding situation is the attractiveness of the financial package offered. Generally, government support in this direction has taken two broad forms. First there is the relaxing of conditions on officially supported export credit for project finance, stipulated by international guidelines. Secondly there is provision of finance for mixed credits – a combination of official export credit plus aid – that is tantamount to a further lowering of average interest rates. The consequence of financial competition is that where it is demanded and the home government is willing to provide financial support and subsidisation of construction services, domestic contractors will be at a significant advantage over contractors of other nationalities who do not receive the same level of support. Seymour[4] illustrates that French and Japanese contractors especially benefit from this country-specific advantage as both countries provide extensive bilateral aid and grants for the provision of mixed credit and tied aid.

International contractors thus compete on more than price. The size of the industry and the nature of the bid and tender system require some means for the firm to differentiate itself in order to win contracts. Given the nature of competitive strategy, the firm will rely upon firm-specific and country-specific factors to reach its differentiation objective.

4.2.2 Internalisation advantages

Ownership advantages such as information, technical knowledge, brand names and managerial expertise are all advantages that could in principle be sold or 'hired out' to firms in other national markets in return for fees or royalties. For international production to take place a second condition of Dunning's approach must thus be satisfied:

Ownership advantages are more advantageously exploited internally by the enterprise rather than externalised by means of selling or licensing those advantages to other firms.

Economic theory suggests that if all markets were perfect, the owner of an advantage could earn the full economic rent for it by selling or licensing in the external market. By 'externalising' the advantage in this way, the owner would maintain full returns on assets without having to incur the additional costs and risks of direct entry to other national markets via international production. Where the internal organisation is preferred (i.e., exploitation of ownership advantages within the firm across national boundaries) the potential costs of externalisation must outweigh the benefits. This implies some market failure such that the asset owner feels that he faces unacceptable risks in selling or licensing the asset in the external market.

The nature of the ownership advantages will determine the choice between external and internal markets. For example, internalisation will generally be preferred where the article to be licensed or sold is a complex combination of the output, image and reputation of the licensor. This type of advantage will typically be embodied in the brand or firm name of the licensor. As such, it is potentially a saleable commodity, but it is clear the 'name' of the firm is a particularly complex commodity. It will in many cases be impossible to distinguish product from image and reputation. As a result if, say, the brand name of a firm were licensed, the licensor would have to maintain quality control of the product. This would have the effect of reducing the potential benefits of licensing for the licensor. Additionally, any underperformance by the licensee would have unfavourable and potentially damaging effects on the licensor. When licensing a brand name, the licensor is thus effectively licensing its own reputation embodied in the product produced under its name.

It can therefore be argued that the more complex the product, or the more intangible the advantage embodied in the firm's name, the more likely it is that ownership advantages will be internalised to reduce the cost of effective quality control and the risk of underperformance by the licensee.

The various internal and external options open to the international contractor in exploiting the firms' ownership advantages may be summarised under three possible modes of market servicing:

Exporting

This involves moving personnel between markets and projects according to demand for the firm's services. The personnel operate from a subsidiary or the firm's headquarters but would not normally work at the main office location. Construction differs from manufacturing in this respect in that in construction the final product is fixed while the production process is mobile. Exporting thus involves the transportation of the production base to the final product until that product is completed.

Licensing

Since the firm's name is an easily transferable property right, instrumental in the winning of a bid in that it differentiates the firm from its competitors, it is likely that if licensing occurs in the industry it will be the firm's name that is licensed.

Foreign direct investment

This involves undertaking production in a foreign country, and as such is similar to exporting. The major difference is that in FDI the personnel are based in a permanent or near permanent subsidiary and work within that market.

Using the theory of internalisation, it can be argued that licensing is not a feasible alternative for international contractors. The threat of underperformance by the licensee is enough to prevent contractors from licensing their names. If the licensee were to underperform (which is likely given that the name is a complex mix of intangible assets that are not transferred with the name), the licensor could suffer unfavourable repercussions not just on that project, but probably well into the future in terms of bidding for subsequent contracts. The underperformance would tarnish the contractor's name, and hence reputation, in the industry.

The chapter by Buckley and Enderwick in this volume (Chapter 8) points to the fact that in many cases the implicit benefits and costs of the internal hierarchy in international construction mean that the production process does not need to be fully internalised by the contractor, but that this need occur only where the factors of production are continually in use by the firm. It is likely that only certain forms of management will form the in-house expertise of the contractor. This can be expected to have two implications in international construction:

1. The contractor may minimise fixed assets abroad, and so reduce the company's exposure to political and commercial risk. This may be of great relevance in international construction since much of the work is in less developed, politically unstable areas.
2. Exporting and FDI are differentiable by the length of time the firm's personnel are in a country. Where markets warrant a degree of FDI but experience fluctuating demand, the firm may 'top up' the local presence of personnel at times of high demand for the firm's services. A similar arrangement may also be made in high risk politically unstable areas where a continual local presence is required. In both cases, the contractor will experience a more efficient use of resources and at the same time lessen risk.

The benefits of partial internalisation of the production process may be considered a consequence of the fact that construction is a service industry. Factors of production additional to management, such as labour, may be partially internalised where necessary to ensure 'the development and maintenance of comparative advantage in tasks',[5] and fully internalised if the factor provides a constant significant ownership advantage. This provides a theoretical justification for the Korean contractors internalising their labour force, since this practice ensures the supply of cheap labour, arguably the Korean contractors' greatest ownership advantage. A similar argument is valid in explaining why contractors in developed countries need internalise only managerial staff. This form of human capital reflects the comparative advantage of these countries, and is their major ownership advantage. Internalisation is thus a means of guaranteeing that the firm remains competitive and, as such, forms an integral part of the eclectic approach.

A second implication of internalisation theory relates to the incidence of joint ventures in international construction. Internalisation theory suggests that joint venture is a feasible option where the firms may benefit from the venture without facing any risk to the enterprises' ownership advantages. In the case of international construction, this implies that joint venture with specialist service contractors will be beneficial because it will increase that firm's probability of winning bids. The joint venture will enhance reputation, improve the specialist services which may be offered, and increase financial resources but at the same time the contractor's major ownership advantage is not threatened. Property rights are clearly and legally assigned, and the nature of joint venture suggests that the contractor may continually check product quality and thereby minimise the potential costs of the venture. This argument is similar to that concerning subcontractors. It does not often apply in manufacturing, and the expectation is therefore of a higher incidence of joint ventures in international contracting than in international manufacturing.

However there are cases in international construction in which the contractor should not consider joint venture: where a contractor has a specific expertise joint venture may lead to a learning process on the part of the lesser specialised partner such that on completion of the project the partner can now become his competitor. Many contractors from the less developed and newly industrialised countries, particularly from the Far East, are willing to become partners in joint ventures so that they may acquire the necessary technical skills to compete in the future with their joint venture partners. The Koreans, for example, have developed their knowledge of nuclear power plant construction through joint venture with contractors in developed countries. The contractor should hence aim to joint venture only where the product and expertise can be safeguarded. In such ventures, while short-run benefits to the specialist stem from having a low cost product, internalisation theory suggests that the long-run threat to the specialist's ownership advantages may outweigh the short term benefits.

4.2.3 Location advantages

If the firm chooses to internalise its advantages, FDI will take place in the Dunning model only if the third condition of the framework is realised:

It is more advantageous for the firm to undertake production outside national borders using internalised ownership advantages than it is to service foreign markets by domestic production and export.

This third condition is probably the simplest of the three. But it is a necessary condition since, if no benefits accrue to the interaction of ownership advantages and the characteristics of a specific location, there is no reason for the firm to enter that foreign market as a producer.

The essence of the argument concerning locational advantages is that the decision of where to produce is determined by the heterogeneity of location attractions or advantages of alternative production sites. Many diverse factors affect the decision of where to produce, including availability of natural resources, and the political, legal and social environment. They vary from country to country and are important to a firm's cost minimisation or profit maximisation policies. As a result, firms will choose to locate in those countries that offer the most appropriate mix of locational advantages, given the nature of ownership advantages. Since firm-specific, industry-specific, and country-specific characteristics determine ownership advantages, locational choice itself will be determined by the relative magnitude of these factors in the overall situation.

In international construction, demand cannot easily be generated by the contractor, for example by advertising or other typical marketing tools used in manufacturing. Hence market demand is a necessary condition of locational choice, though it is not a sufficient one. Determination of market will generally come down to the interaction of home and host country factors of the contractor.

The implication of the interaction of ownership and locational advantages is that different nationality contractors are likely to locate in different regions according to the nature of their ownership advantages. This may provide greater exploitation of existing ownership advantage, or lead to the generation of new advantages, than are accounted for within the Dunning model.

4.3 POLICY IMPLICATIONS

The policy implications arising from the Dunning framework have been widely acted upon by the major UK international contracting firms. These policy implications may be summarised as follows:

1. An overall corporate strategy on overseas operations is of vital importance, and it should be based on differentiation of products in overseas markets.
2. Ownership advantages must be relevant to the region where the firm chooses to operate and given the nature of the contractor's product, a combination of exporting and FDI in any one market may be beneficial.
3. More use should be made of joint ventures and consortia of contractors in developed countries.
4. Contractors should take advantage of the international expertise of UK manufacturing firms and of the London financial markets to generate demand for their services.
5. They should also bring their successful performance to the attention of UK consultants, so that the latter may utilise UK contractors without abandoning their impartial advice to clients.
6. The UK government should assist UK contractors by providing a larger budget for mixed credit and tied aid components of export credit deals, by encouraging more use of Commonwealth links and matching other countries support measures. It would also help to foster greater cooperation and less competition amongst UK contractors in work abroad.

Useful practical examples of the recommendations outlined above are met in other countries. They include the concentration of French contractors in the African market, West Germany's foreign aid agreement, political and trade agreements negotiated by France and South Korea, and by the USA through defence and other political facilities. Many French contractors also obtain work through French consultants acting as advisers on projects.

NOTES AND REFERENCES

*   This chapter is based on a paper 'International Investment in the Construction Industry: An Application of the Eclectic Approach by Seymour, H., Flanagan, R. and Norman G., (University of Reading Discussion Papers in International Investment and Business Studies, No. 87 (July 1985).

1. Dunning, J. H., *International Production and the Multinational Enterprise* (London: George Allen & Unwin, 1981), and Dunning, J. H., 'The Eclectic Paradigm; An Update and a Reply to the Critics', unpublished paper (1985).
2. Hymer, S. H., *The International Operations of National Firms; a study of Direct Foreign Investment* (Cambridge: Mass.: MIT Press, 1976).
3. Porter, M. E., *Competitive Advantage: Creating and Sustaining Superior Performance* (New York: Free Press, 1985).
4. Seymour, H. D., *The Multinational Construction Industry* (London: Croom Helm, 1987).
5. Casson, M. C., 'Transactions Costs and the Theory of the Multinational Enterprise', in Rugman, A. M. (ed.), *New Theories of the Multinational Enterprise* (London: Croom Helm, 1982).

Editors' Bridging Commentary

As in all industries, the correct financial strategy follows from the strategy of the firm, but at the same time may itself facilitate or preclude certain courses of action. In construction, where the type of product and the process usually adopted mean that fixed assets are low, cash flow has a greater significance. Turnover, and hence profits, are more volatile and lumpy than in most other industries. The appropriate financial strategy is different from that in other sectors, but just as important.

Chapter 5 must be seen as closely connected to overall business strategy, diversification policy and to international contracting where the risks are considerably greater than in other operations. At a more micro level, it should be considered in the context of pricing policy which obviously affects, and is affected by, the financial policy of the firm.

5 Financial Strategy[*]

Jacqueline Cannon and Patricia M. Hillebrandt

5.1 INTRODUCTION

Contracting is a service which is related to individual projects each one of which may be likened to a firm with a relatively short and finite life. In the short term, the number of projects which a firm can undertake is more or less fixed by its management or skills capacity, and it is usually found that relatively few projects account for the major part of the operations of the firm. If one project fails, for whatever reason, the effect can thus be very damaging to the overall health of the firm. This is especially so because the potential loss is a very high proportion of total turnover, and hence of the total resources of the firm.

In this chapter some theories of the financial management of large firms are examined, followed in each case by a consideration of how far they apply to the behaviour of construction firms.

5.2 OBJECTIVES

The traditional theory of the firm suggests that it maximises profits. However, modern approaches emphasise the divorce of ownership from control of the firm, and suggest that managers ought to aim at maximising the benefits to shareholders.

On the other hand, some theories acknowledge that the personal interests of the managers in fact determine the objectives of the firm. While in some very large companies with share option schemes the personal interests of managers and shareholders can be made to approximate to each other, in most cases they do not necessarily do so.

There are various approaches which have been adopted by economic theorists to deal with this situation. They include assumptions of sales maximisation or a combination of sales and profits, the aim of a satisfactory level of profit – not necessarily maximum – combined with other benefits including a trouble free existence for managers known as 'satisficing' and more recently the objective of job security for managers. It is also acknowledged that non-financial goals such as power, prestige and status are important to managers.

All these 'non-traditional' goals require a reasonable level of profit to ensure the long run existence of the firm. Whether managers choose profit maximisation or a maximisation of benefits to shareholders, the achievement of either assists in the achievement of another objective, namely that of the growth of the firm.

Shareholders are interested in income and capital gains, and their preferences for one or the other vary according to individual circumstances and their attitudes to risk. Because any one shareholder has a small voice in most companies it is the stock market which determines the value of the shares. In the long run there is no clash between high income and high capital value because any company which produces high profits will have a high share value. In the short run, however, high profits may be 'bought' at the expense of future profits and growth.

In any case, in most companies, profits fluctuate from year to year and one of the factors which influence the stock exchange valuation is a steady and rising stream of dividends. The nature of the contract based work, and hence the incidence and level of profits in the construction firms, suggest that it may be more difficult for them to ensure that dividends follow a smooth and rising trend.

Another factor to be considered by the company is that if the share price falls too low in relation to an outsider's assessment of the potential value of the company or its assets, then there is a danger that an offer will be made to shareholders to purchase the company. The outside assessment may be different from that of the stock market, because the outsider foresees the possibility of higher returns either by improved management or by more effective use of assets. It is also possible that the firm's accounting methods may fail to recognise the current value of its assets; this is ignored by the stock market until a likely predator emerges. The danger of a takeover is an incentive for managers to maximise profits.

In a situation where there is control of the company through share ownership by an individual, a trust or a group of individuals with common interest in the continued independence of the firm, takeovers are effectively prevented and the share price is of lesser significance.

5.3 REQUIREMENTS FOR FINANCE

Firms require finance in the short term to bridge the gap between expenditure and income flows, and this need is normally met by overdraft facilities. Firms also require longer term finance for growth. The sources for this long term finance determine the costs of capital and also influence how much investment can be undertaken. Replacement of assets should be financed from depreciation but in recent times, due to technological advance, the rate of obsolescence has increased so that the depreciation fund may be insufficient to finance replacement, which may thus also lead to requirements for additional finance. For construction firms, which often operate in a number of different markets, the more specific requirements for finance are set out in the matrix in Table 5.1 below.

It is usual to finance working capital and stock and work in progress as well as short term liabilities, which do not directly contribute to the growth of the firm, from overdraft facilities. These needs are inherently different from those which are essential inputs to growth – that is plant, equipment and buildings – and other assets and risk ventures. The key constituents of the construction industry may be categorised and defined as follows:

Contracting

The central process of organising the economic factors of production (labour, plant, materials) on site and of managing those factors so as to erect or construct buildings and other structures according to the instructions (e.g., design, quality, timing or other specifications) set out by the client.

Housebuilding

The speculative acquisition of land and development of homes for sale or rent.

Plant hire

The provision of capital equipment and machinery, usually with servicing, maintenance and operating personnel, in return for rental and hire charges.

Materials production

The manufacture and sale of building materials, both directly to site and through distributors such as merchants, factors or retailers.

Table 5.1 Finance required by various types of business

Purpose of Finance	Contracting	House-building	Plant hire	Materials production	Mining	Property development	Property investment
Working capital	1	2	2	2	2	2	2
Speculative stocks & WIP	–	3	–	2	1	3	3
Stocks ordered & WIP	1	1	1	1	1	1	–
Unexpected liabilities	3	1	2	1	3	–	2
Operating assets other than land	–	1	3	3	3	–	3
New ventures	–	1	–	2	1	2	2
Land	–	3	–	–	2	3	–

Notes:
WIP = Work in progress.
The numbers from 1 to 3 indicate the relative importance of requirements of finance for each type of business:
1 = low.
2 = medium.
3 = high.

Mining

The exploitation of natural resources below ground either in their own land or on behalf of an owner.

Property development

The speculative acquisition of land and or buildings, and subsequent development, refurbishment or conversion into commercial and industrial premises for letting and/or sale to funding institutions or occupiers.

Property investment

The accumulation of a portfolio of residential or non-residential buildings, from which income is earned through rents.

The definitions of the various purposes for which finance is required are as follows:

Working capital

The net balance of cash which is both routinely required to meet the essential weekly/monthly bills (e.g., wages and salaries, rents, other overheads) and occasionally required to meet unexpected liabilities which cannot be deferred (e.g., repairing premises' defects, rectifying production errors, settling lost contract disputes with clients). A distinction is made here, although this may seem more fastidious than most accounting definitions, between 'working capital' in this sense of mostly overhead contingencies and 'working capital' in the sense of raw materials, finished and semi-finished goods.

Speculative stocks and work in progress (WIP)

Stocks of raw materials and finished goods, as well as work in progress, for which neither payment nor final orders have been received.

Stocks ordered and work in progress

Stocks of raw materials, finished goods and work in progress, for which specific orders have been received.

Unexpected liabilities

Liabilities which arise irregularly and unexpectedly, excluding those directly connected with an increase in speculative stocks.

Operating assets

Plant, machinery, buildings and other operating assets from the exploitation of which the firm expects to gain a stream of benefits in future years.

New ventures

The allocation of capital sums for new ventures, often in uncharted product and market areas.

Land

Land for current and future development.

It is clear from Table 5.1 that there are great differences between contracting and all the other types of business (as listed in Table 5.1) undertaken by construction companies. Contracting requires virtually no assets, very little capital for stocks and work in progress or for working capital. The reasons are that contractors obtain their finance from the client, the subcontractors, and the suppliers.

The finance from the client comes from the advance payments for mobilisation on site. The contractor is then paid by stages based on the monthly certificate of the consultant who makes a small percentage retention. This retention, normally of 5 per cent, is paid some time after the completion of the project. There are few industries where such advance and stage payments are made. The contractor employs subcontractors, and under the normal contractual arrangements he pays them for work done often on a stage basis. In these circumstances, and if everything goes smoothly, the contractor will not have to pay the subcontractor until he himself has been paid. To cover himself in case the proper procedures are not adopted by the client the main contractor will often insert in the subcontract that the subcontractor will not get paid till the contractor is paid.

It is traditional and hence normal practice for builders' merchants to allow some credit to contractors which at some periods has been as much as three months though it is now considerably less. This means that contractors are usually paid for work done and material incorporated in the project before they pay for materials.

In general the contractor thus is able to receive monies for work done before he pays out for the various inputs. Moreover skilful pricing of the bill of quantities by, for example, putting in a higher price for items in the early stages of the construction process enables him to shift some of his receipts to an earlier stage in the construction period. It follows that with careful management a contractor can generate a positive cash flow and either obtain interest or invest in capital-hungry businesses such as the others listed in Table 5.1, in particular housebuilding and property.

Another important characteristic of contracting is that it requires very little fixed capital. The site belongs to the client, the plant may be hired and the buildings on site are minimal and in any case part of the project cost. The growth of a contracting company is thus not as dependent on the availability of finance as it is for most other types of business.

Lastly there is a difference in the very high danger of unexpected liabilities. It has already been explained that one contract may constitute a high proportion of the total business of a contractor. Because the contracting firm is management intensive, management failure may be very costly and damaging to the reputation of the firm and its future profitability. Moreover technical problems, long litigation with clients, political problems on work overseas and so on can similarly adversely affect the profitability of contracting. Lack of assets makes a contracting firm more vulnerable to such failures because it has no reserves to fall back on.

5.4 SOURCES OF FINANCE AND CAPITAL STRUCTURE

The sources of long term finance for purchase of operating assets and the growth and evolution of the business are either internal or external. The internal ones are obtained from a positive cash flow and retained profits. The external ones are equity, bonds and other long term loan arrangements. Finance is sometimes also made available by government. The short term sources of finance are bank overdrafts and short term loans. The emphasis in this section is on long term finance because of its importance to the asset base and growth of firms.

The existing capital structure of the firm determines the changes which managers can bring about. Any new capital structure should contribute to the goals of the firm and managers therefore do not have complete freedom in their selection of quantity, sources and mix of finance.

There are three important ratios to be considered in the capital structure of the firm. The first is the debt–equity ratio, that is the proportion of debt to equity in the total assets of the firm, sometimes known as leverage. The second ratio is that of dividend cover, that is the number of times a dividend is covered by a company's earnings after payment of interest and corporate taxes. The dividend cover determines the third ratio, namely the retention ratio, which is the proportion of earnings to be retained for financing future investment projects. The first is dealt with in this section and the second and third in Section 5.5 below.

A number of models have been developed with the aim of establishing an optimal capital structure under various assumptions, the two major ones being that of maximising shareholder wealth and managerial job security.[1] On the whole these models offer little practical advice to managers. There are however some useful comments which can be made about the factors which are likely to affect the financing decisions of the firm.

There are limits to the amount of debt which a firm can safely contract. Any debt involves an undertaking to pay interest; if this cost is lower than the earnings from the use of the capital then the shareholders benefit. If, on the other hand, it is greater, for any reason, than the earnings from the capital, then there is a drain on profits which is obviously detrimental to shareholders. The greater the risk of earnings falling, the greater is the danger to the firm of a high debt–equity ratio.

In the real world, two measures have been established which enable managers to assess and monitor the effect of different financing policies on their own welfare and that of the shareholders. They are the EPS–EBIT analysis (Earnings per Share – Total Earnings Before Interest and Taxes) and the Cash Flow analysis.[2]

The EPS–EBIT analysis assumes that investors are interested only in earnings per share – that is, the yield of their investments. The EPS–EBIT approach seeks to assess the earnings per share at various levels of total earnings (EBIT) under different financing policies. The usefulness of the analysis lies in showing the following important determinants of actual debt–equity ratios. They are: (a) the absolute amount of earnings, (b) the height of the corporate tax rate, (c) the attitude of managers to risk, (d) the initial capital structure, and (e) the amount of additional funds required. The main weaknesses of the approach are that it ignores the risk element in investment decisions and in the basic assumption that investors are interested only in the earnings per share and ignore the risk element in their decisions.

Cash flow analysis estimates total earnings before interest and taxes (EBIT) and requires a forecast of cash receipts (inflows) and cash payments (outflows). The difference between inflows and outflows is total earnings (EBIT) from which fixed costs have to be met.

Cash flow analysis is usually based on a single set of assumptions concerning the external business environment of the firm and circumstances particular to the markets in which it operates.

The cash flow analysis itself should, however, include forecasts of cash inflows and outflows based on different assumptions ranging, for example, from severe recession to very rapid growth, or based on different interest rates.

The forecasts, which must obviously also take into account subjective probabilities about the 'state of business', give probability distributions of earnings for each period. With this information, managers can assess the level of fixed costs and debt which the firm can undertake without risking insolvency. Since cash flow analysis ignores the danger of having nothing left over for dividends after meeting fixed charges, it is most useful for internal purposes.

These types of analysis may be used to help managers make decisions whether they are trying to maximise shareholders' benefits or have some other objectives. It is claimed that managers consider that job security may be endangered if the firm's leverage deviates in the long run from that which is typical of the industry. They set the firm's target debt–equity ratio on the accepted ratio for firms of similar size and characteristics.

However the debt–equity ratio is not determined only by the preferences of the firm itself; it is also related to the willingness of lenders to supply capital to the firm. The lenders' assessment will be determined by factors similar to those of the prudent firm, but they may not always coincide. More detailed factors affecting the debt–equity ratio are discussed below.[3]

The rate of growth of earnings

Managers tend to prefer internal funds to external sources of capital. A high growth rate of earnings implies more funds from retained earnings and less used for external finance. A negative relationship may thus exist between the rate of growth of earnings and the ratio of debt to equity.

The retention policy of managers

The level of internal funds also depends on the retention ratio, which itself depends on the growth potential of the firm and on managers' skill in convincing shareholders about the profitability of investment opportunities. As a high proportion of retained earnings obviously lowers the need for external financing, the retention ratio is likely to be negatively related to the debt–equity ratio.

Degree of concentration of ownership and voting control

If share ownership is concentrated in a few hands, managers may be wary of issuing new shares since it could change voting control by existing shareholders and thus weaken their job security. In this case, the relationship between voting control concentration and leverage is likely to be negative.

Credit limits (debt capacity)

Creditors' attitudes constrain managers' ability to adjust the actual leverage to its target level. Lenders in the capital market are said to define the debt capacity of firms, which is the level of 'safe' borrowing by the firm. Creditors' views about debt capacity are based on a number of variables which include the size of the firm, its potential growth, its business risk and asset structure.

1. *The size of the firm* Large firms are able to borrow funds more easily and on better terms than small ones. This may be because creditors think that larger firms are less likely to become insolvent. Size is here therefore positively related to leverage. However, raising equity finance is also easier for large firms than small firms and hence they have a choice. It is possible that large firms may prefer to rely on retained earnings rather than take advantage of the larger loanable funds available. Evidence shows that since the Second World War retained earnings have become the major source of finance for large firms.
2. *The growth of the size of assets* The growth of assets indicates the future development potential of a firm. It also reflects the total requirement for funds. A positive relationship is therefore postulated between the growth of assets and the debt–equity ratio, though again the asset growth could be finalised from retained earnings.
3. *Business risk* Business risk is related to variability of earnings and lenders are more willing to provide funds to firms with relatively stable earnings, as unstable earnings raise the risk of insolvency. Job security also influences managers' use of debt and where earnings are stable, a more liberal use of debt is possible, since the fixed costs of debt can be met regularly. Here, variability

of earnings is likely to be negatively related to the debt–equity ratio.

4. *Capital intensity* Capital intensive techniques have high fixed costs which are difficult to reduce when demand falls, and hence they increase the instability of profits. However, it is easier to borrow against the security of fixed assets. Capital intensive techniques are hence positively related to the debt–equity ratio.

The cost of debt

Debt has a direct cost – interest payments – and an indirect one – since it increases the cost of equity capital. The higher the cost of debt, the less appealing it becomes.

The cost of equity financing

The price of shares reflects the cost of equity financing. Share price increases lead to expectations of 'cheap' equity financing since at higher prices a share issue will raise more funds, and make debt financing relatively less attractive. A fall in share price will obviously have the opposite effect. A change in share price is therefore expected to be negatively related to the debt–equity ratio.

The corporate tax rate

The tax deductibility of interest payments is a feature of the appeal of debt financing and the corporate tax rate (taking into account the tax credit on dividends) and the debt–equity ratio are thus positively related.

Inflation expectations

Inflation expectations affect lenders and debtors in opposite ways. Managers may prefer debt financing, in an inflationary situation, as the repayment of debt falls in real terms, in line with the fall in the real purchasing power of money. Creditors may be reluctant to offer funds in those conditions, unless interest rates are high enough. What is important is whether anticipated inflation is incorporated in the current interest rates. If interest rates are low relative to inflation there is an incentive to borrow and to adjust the debt–equity ratio upwards; this of course may raise interest rates. On the whole, it is expected that the relationship between the rate of inflation and the debt–equity ratio will be positive.

Shortage of loanable funds

Government monetary and fiscal policies influence the availability of debt financing and its cost, and they imply a negative relationship between a shortage of funds and leverage.

Table 5.2 summarises the various financial factors which affect the debt–equity ratio.

Table 5.2 Relationship of various financial factors to debt–equity ratio

Factor	Relation to debt–equity ratio
1 Rate of growth of earnings	Negative
2 Retention percentage	Negative
3 Concentration of ownership and control	Positive
4a Size of firms	Positive (but may not take advantage of it)
4b Growth in assets	Positive
4c Business risk & earnings variability	Negative
4d Capital intensity	Positive
5 Cost of debt	Negative
6 Share prices	Negative
7 Corporate tax rate	Positive
8 Inflation expectations	Positive
9 Shortage of loanable funds	Negative

Notes:
Negative = factors move in opposite directions – e.g., a high rate of growth of earnings leads to a lower debt–equity ratio.
Positive = factors move in the same direction.

5.5   DIVIDEND POLICY

Dividend retention policy involves a number of interrelated issues. It has led to the development of several theories which assume that the goal of managers is to maximise the value of the firm to its original shareholders. The main debate on which these theories centre is whether the dividend retention decision influences the price of shares through its effect on investors' assessment of the discount rate to be applied to the firm's future stream of earnings.[4]

The major determinants of the dividend decision which are illuminated in those theories are briefly detailed below.[5]

The typical dividend of the industry

The managerial theory of the firm suggests that managers cannot ignore the dividend policy of rival firms without endangering their job security. The firm's long run dividend policy has thus to mirror that which is typical for the industry.

The growth of earnings

If earnings grow over time, dividend payments will be increased. Higher earnings enable higher dividends to be made and a higher level of retained earnings.

Stability of earnings

Widely fluctuating earnings make managers reluctant to increase dividends for fear of not being able to maintain the increase in all periods. Instability of earnings increases risk for shareholders, and will have an adverse effect on share prices.

Available investment opportunities

Managers tend to prefer retained earnings as a source of funds, and this is particularly true of those in large firms. The two major reasons put forward are that retained earnings have no cash cost to the firm and that they increase the power of management in large firms and conglomerates. If this is so the greater the investment opportunities, the greater the need for funds and the greater the likelihood of a greater proportion of earnings being retained.

The expected yield on investment opportunities

If the expected yield on new investment is high, shareholders will accept a lower dividend because they will expect the price of their shares to rise, and hence capital gains, because of the favourable effect of those high yield investments.

The availability and cost of alternative sources of funds

Internal finance may be inadequate to the finance needs of fast growing firms. Moreover, the attractiveness of retained earnings will vary relative to that of external funds. For example, when monetary policy is expansionary, low interest rates may make external borrowings more attractive than retained earnings. The cost of alternative sources of funds, whether debt or new equity, is expected to have an effect on the dividend policy of the firm in the short term.

Shareholders' performance

Different groups of shareholders will have different retention and dividend preferences. High income investors will tend to favour retentions because capital gains are taxed less heavily than dividends. Institutional investors and some individuals may prefer high dividends where they are an important source of income. With high brokerage fees, and other inconveniences in changing portfolios, many investors may prefer dividends to capital gains. The ability of managers to retain more profits than shareholders would like depends on their power. The discretionary power of managers is universally related to share ownership dispersion.

Expectations about inflation

The effects of inflation on dividends are varied. Their net effect will depend on their relative strengths, and the relationship between dividends and inflation cannot therefore be predicted.

Restrictions by creditors

Creditors usually insist on setting limits to the amount of earnings which can be paid out in dividends, in order to protect the servicing of the debt. This is not important for large firms and conglomerates where earnings are usually much higher than the creditors' 'safe level'.

5.6 MEASURES OF FINANCIAL PERFORMANCE

Any company needs to be able to assess the performance of various parts of its business in relation to the other parts. Indeed, such an assessment is an important part of the development of a corporate strategy. The most usual measure of performance for most businesses is return on capital employed (ROCE) though others, notably return on turnover, are also used.

In the case of construction companies with a diversity of businesses, such as is shown in Table 5.1, there are great difficulties in making a useful comparison from one business to another. Contracting operations may imply negative capital so that on this basis return on capital employed becomes infinite. Yet clearly this does not mean that it is necessarily more beneficial to the total firm than its other businesses. Return on turnover is also not a good measure of performance, even when used to compare one contracting type operation with another, because so much depends on how much is subcontracted and on the risks of various operations.

Theoretically the assessment should be based on the return to the scarce resource or resources. In contracting, it is arguable that the scarce resource which limits the expansion of the business is management expertise. In this case, the return on scarce managers who are difficult to replace should be considered as the criterion. There is a body of theory on the fringes of accounting and economics known as human resource accounting which seems to apply this idea.[6] It is however at the moment extremely difficult to use, and is probably applicable only in broad terms. This does not solve the problem of comparing management intensive and capital intensive businesses.

Failing any appropriate measure to apply across all types of business undertaken by a construction company or across markets within contracting, the assessment must perforce be made by a consideration of a number of indicators including return on capital, return on turnover and the absolute level of profit made by each operation.

5.7 CONSEQUENCES OF SPECIAL FINANCIAL CONTRACTING FEATURES

The consequences of the special financial features of contracting for the way in which firms in the contracting industry behave are substantial.

The most important features are the positive cash flow for projects and the fact that the solid assets are minimal. These together have the following effects:

1. The move towards diversification into other non-contracting businesses, in order to:

   (a) use the cash available effectively to generate profit from other businesses; it is partly this reason that the businesses into which contractors move can be cash-hungry businesses where land is required as one of the inputs;

   (b) create assets as a collateral for loans;

(c) provide a stable source of income over time by going into businesses not necessarily related to the construction cycles.

2. The virtual non-existence of financial barriers to entry to the industry.
3. The ability of family firms to survive in the business, even in very large companies because in the contracting business they do not have to seek new capital for expansion from their shareholders which a family would probably be unable to supply.
4. The attraction of contracting companies to conglomerates who can use the positive cash flow and do not have to seek additional sources of finance.
5. The feasibility of arranging a management buy-out.

These five factors in their turn affect the mix of types of firms within the construction industry. They may be classified first into those with satellite companies, see 1 above, and those where a firm undertakes mainly contracting. Each of these may be grouped according to ownership:

(i) Owned by other company – see 4 above.
(ii) Wide public ownership.
(iii) Family control – remarkably prevalent in contracting – see 3 above.
(iv) Management buy-out – see 5 above.

The emphasis on criteria of performance for each of these ownership types may well be rather different, as may also that of different firms within the same group, but the variation is unlikely to be so great that any firm or ownership type falls outside the range of objectives discussed at the beginning of this chapter.

NOTES AND REFERENCES

*   The authors are indebted to Jamie Stevenson, Director (Research), Kleinwort Grieveson Securities Ltd, for his contribution to Section 5.3 of this chapter. They wish to thank Professor Alan Evans, University of Reading, and Mr Anthony Carey, Under Secretary, Accounting Standards Committee, for helpful comments.

Sections 5.4 and 5.5 have been strongly influenced by the work of the late A. Koutsoyiannis, and the authors are grateful for the insights it has provided.

1.   See for example Koutsoyiannis, A., 'Managerial Job Security and the Capital Structure of Firms', *Manchester School* Vol. 46, No. 1 (1978) pp. 51–75 and Marris, R., *The Economic Theory of Managerial Capitalism* (London: Macmillan, 1964).

2.   The categories are based on Koutsoyiannis, A., *Non-Price Decisions: The Firm in a Modern Context* (London: Macmillan, 1982) pp. 400–4.

3.   Koutsoyiannis (1982) (see note 2).

4.   For detailed exposition of these theories see Miller, M. and Modigliani, F., 'Dividend Policy, Growth and the Valuation of Shares', *Journal of Business*, Vol. 34, No. 4 (1961) pp. 411–33 on the one hand, and on the other three articles by Gordon and one by Lintner: Gordon, M. J., 'Dividends, Earnings and Share Prices', *Review of Economics and Statistics*, Vol. 41, No. 2 (1959) pp. 99–105; Gordon, M. J., 'The Savings, Investment and Valuation of a Corporation', *Review of Economics and Statistics*, Vol. 44, No. 1 (1962) pp. 37–51; Gordon, M. J., 'Optimal Investment and Financing Policy', *Journal of Finance*, Vol. 18, No. 2 (1963) pp. 264–72; and Lintner, J., 'Dividends, Earnings, Leverage, Stock Prices and the Supply of Capital to Corporations', *Review of Economics and Statistics*, Vol. 44, No. 3 (1962) pp. 243–69. There are a number of discussions of the merits of these two schools, including that in Koutsoyiannis (1982) (see note 2) Chapter 9.

5.   Based on Koutsoyiannis (1982) (see note 2) pp. 438–41.

6.   Czarsty, S. L., 'An In-depth Analysis of Human Resource Accounting with Emphasis on the Basis for Measuring the Value of Human Resources', The George Washington University Dissertation for Doctor of Business Administration 1975 (Ann Arbor, Michigan: Xerox University Microfilms, 1975).

Editors' Bridging Commentary

The industry is extremely complex in the way in which the construction process is organised.

Chapter 6 stresses the importance of ensuring that the structure of the organisation and its methods of communication are appropriate to the types of information which have to be used in the various stages of the construction process. It is argued that competiton will eliminate firms which depart from the appropriate structure and processes.

The logical method outlined to assess the appropriateness of the structure is applicable at any level of the firm. The operation of any group carrying out an identifiable task may be examined within the framework put forward. The firm is thus able to consider any changes which would improve the handling and use of information, whether that be of a routine and stable nature or unique and volatile.

6 Social Technology and Structure

Peter Clark

6.1 INTRODUCTION

There are a number of theoretical approaches to the analysis of the structure and processes of establishments and firms which are known variously as organisation theory, organisation studies and the theory of behaviour. In this chapter, the theory of social technology has been selected as being of greatest relevance to the construction industry. It is a theory which has been formed by a selective fusing of elements from management theory, economics, engineering and the social sciences. Its prime objective is to provide a framework for prescribing those forms of work organisation which are most likely to be viable in different contexts. The theory is rational and analytical, and it assumes that firms which depart from the theoretically appropriate recipe will be eliminated through market competition. The theory is therefore prescriptive and explanatory, albeit in a limited way. The version to be used relies particularly on the notion of social technology by Perrow (see Section 6.5.1). The theory can be used to explore the impact of innovation and the implications which innovation might have for the learning of skills.

6.2 MARKET VARIABILITY AND STRUCTURE

Theoretically, through its structure, a firm should have a relationship to its market environment which optimises its position in the market.[1] In Figure 6.1 the relationship between market variability and the structure of the firm is explored.

Structure is shown in the right-hand side of Figure 6.1 as containing at least three basic, independent factors: the degree to which procedures are formalised in written documents, the extent to which decision making is devolved or centralised, and the degree of role specialisation. Each requires brief amplification.

Firstly, in Britain during much of the 20th century managements

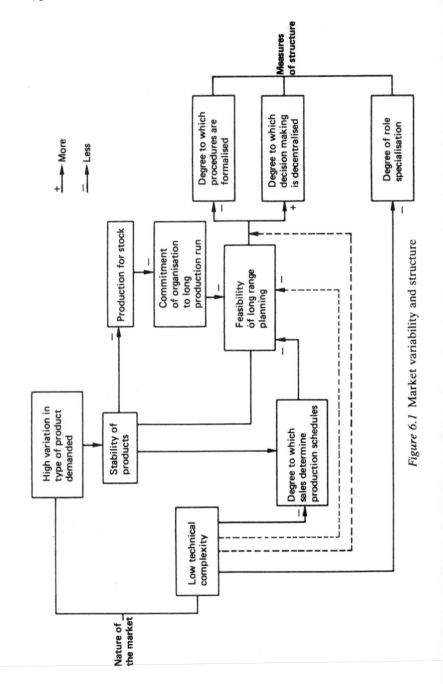

Figure 6.1 Market variability and structure

have tended to make relatively less use of formal, written procedures, contracts and specifications than in the USA; communication was more often verbal and unrecorded. Yet all theories of organisation lay great stress on the part played by formal records in the 'organisation memory' and their potential for providing a reflective view on the past which can guide the future. Weber's[2] seminal analysis of positive and inhibiting functions of bureaucracy is a key influence on this factor.

Secondly, centralisation may be measured in a variety of ways. The easily used Aston Programme[3] provides a listing of 37 varied and important decision areas. The degree of centrality of decision making can be calculated by discovering at which of six vertical levels each of these decisions is actually taken, and then cumulating the scores.

Thirdly, occupational roles may be generalised or specialised. For example, if executives in the staff functions, often known as the technostructure,[4] undertake only a narrow range of tasks, as is often the case in Anglo–American industrial corporations, then there is likely to be a high degree of specialisation. In other words, the division of labour amongst executives would be relatively well developed and functions would be segmented. The practice of highly developed, segmented executive strata developed in the USA in the early part of the 20th century and spread to British industrial firms in the 1960s. Similarly, role specialisation at the site level refers to the extent to which non-managerial employees undertake a small range of tasks.

Structure considered in terms of these three factors may be taken as one set of variables, but if structural variations are important and consequential then what are the variables that 'drive' the choice of the ideal structure? Theoretical treatments of organisation design such as the highly cogent and well illustrated handbook of Jay R. Galbraith[5] and empirical studies have been interpreted as showing that the inputs from the market place are crucial. Particular attention is given to the variability of product which a corporation has to create. In general, these products would be goods or services, and in construction they are tangible items like roads, power stations and houses. So, as the top left-hand corner of Figure 6.1 indicates, the objects might be highly variable or highly standardised. For example, the millions of underwear garments sold across the counters of a well known retailer are of careful design but low variability, whilst the design of négligés is more inventive and variable.

We should note that the construction industry claims that all its products are highly customised – that is, highly variable – but customised relative to what? In order to be able to use Figure 6.1 appropriately it is necessary to develop a scale of variability which is coherent and portable. In construction, a first stab at this task could be to regard speculative housebuilding, roads and power stations as three benchmarks of increasing variability. However, this question requires more attention because it is suggested that the degree of variability in construction is somewhat less than is often claimed.

6.3 MULTIPLE STRUCTURES

All large construction firms operate in two rather distinct time frames. First there are the on-going sites where projects are in various stages of completion. These activities reflect past decisions and previous conceptions of best practice within the firm. Second there are planning activities amongst top decision makers and in the technostructure which are concerned with a present–future time frame.

The question which arises is whether these different activities should be managed with the same structure, or whether the whole firm should shift its structure periodically to incorporate innovation? At one time it was thought that firms should change their structures periodically, and this became known as the dual-structure theory.[6] However, following a series of longitudinal studies of strategic innovation it became apparent that large firms possess repertoires of multiple structures[7] such that some structures in the repertoire would be dormant for long periods.

Figure 6.2 gives a schematic presentation of a multiple structure suggesting that at least two quite different structures coexist within the same firm: one handles the present execution (see lower part of Figure 6.2) whilst the other handles the future. In construction this future oriented structure will culminate in the activity of obtaining commissions to do work. Clearly the parallel structures in Figure 6.2 require linkages, and this is indicated through the translation stage during which future site management is briefed.

Another approach is to think of the whole structure as a series of substructures or layers from the direct operating units through site and project management and the technostructure, the top layer taking decisions such as choice of market and financial objectives. Each of these layers would comprise a number of work units, and the

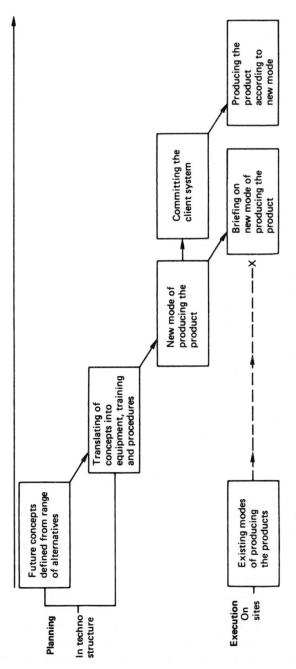

Figure 6.2 Tasks, time and location of responsibility for planning the future.

higher up in the firm the more the work units are involved with long term issues rather than the present time frame. The theoretical assumption is that any of the work units in each layer may and should possess different structures yet all are integrated in the total structure.[8]

In practice, managements have to discover the most appropriate structures to achieve the correct structure at the level of the work unit and of the firm as a whole.[9]

6.4 PROCESSES OF CHANGE

Organisation theory has been most powerful in the production of structural blueprints for the ideal design of jobs and organisations. Such an approach tends to neglect the practical problems of change, innovation and internal politics. For example, past research indicates that firms tend to acquire key influential structural features in their founding period, and that these become constituted into a repertoire which is difficult to alter. This problem became very evident in the merger which created British Leyland[10] and will be well known to construction firms which have acquired new subsidiaries through financial takeovers. The issues raised by these problems extend beyond this chapter, yet one basic point may be made.

Any approach to the study of a process should distinguish between two kinds of change: recurrence and transformational change. Recurrence, which is the most prevalent form of change, consists of the repetition of activities over varying time scales. For example, in supermarket operation there is a remarkable degree of variability in trading through the days of the week and within each day, yet successive weeks possess a high degree of similarity. Recurrence is the neglected Achilles heel of change theories, simply because the fact of recurrence tends to create learning experiences and an organisational memory which integrates individuals into systems. The systems are entrained to triggering events which become so anticipated that, even when they have disappeared, individuals continue with old behaviours, activities and attitudes.

Transformation refers to the alteration of recurrent patterns, both deliberate (quite rare) and unintentional (more often). There are many sources of potential transformation. In construction, these can arise from changes in the expectations of clients, concepts of architecture, raw materials, methods of construction, equipment and in the activities of specialist information services for the industry.

6.5 SOCIAL TECHNOLOGY

6.5.1 The US and UK theories and their synthesis

The analyses in the following sections provide some of the building blocks of the particular theory of organisation or structure known as social technology. This has its origins in two separate and parallel approaches in the USA and in Britain.

The American contribution is from the Carnegie School whose members began, in the mid-1950s, to develop a theory of organising in which the individual's capacity to process information was taken as the point of departure.[11] Contrary to *a priori* assumptions of neo-classical economics which assumed that individuals could collect and process wide amounts of data about prices and potential contracts, the Carnegie approach assumed that individuals select information only in a very narrow way. It is contended that individuals possess their own hypotheses about cause–effect relations in the external world, and that these hypotheses shape the selection of stimuli to which they respond. Further, individuals in large firms tend to become influenced by the local normative frameworks in their own small segment or work unit. Their view of the world becomes shaped by local hypotheses, hence when they make decisions about means–ends relationships, their rationality is bounded and is subjectively bounded. This is known as bounded rationality.

In firms, rationally bounded individuals have to work with each other. According to the Carnegie approach there is a continuum of situations which face collaborating individuals, ranging from situations which are well known to all of them and are easily encoded to situations which are largely novel. In the former, individuals can develop rules and plans which anticipate required actions and which can be used to coordinate their actions.

This is routine social technology. In contrast, the novel situations (in the short run) require a much more flexible approach to developing a plan of action because the cause–effect relationships are irregular and hidden. Coordination is therefore through continual, iterative interaction in which the internal power relations rarely become hierarchised or centralised. This is the non-routine social technology.

A complementary development of similar principles evolved from the empirical researches undertaken in Britain.[12] It was Perrow[13] who synthesised these two perspectives and laid the ground for developments of organisation design as a prescriptive theory of information processing later developed by Jay R. Galbraith.[14] The analysis below is based on this synthesised approach.

6.5.2 The work unit

The first step is to examine the work unit and the inputs to it. The horizontal dimension of Figure 6.3 scales the degree to which information inputs are perceived as being uniform and stable, and the vertical dimension scales the degree to which the information embedded in the input was understood. Combining these two dimensions should locate a work unit in one quadrant. To take an example of the tendering process, if the components in the process are seen as erratic and diverse – i.e., non-uniform and unstable – and the business of putting together a bid is not well understood, then the inputs to the work units would be in quadrant 1. If on the other hand the components can be examined and categorised into a number of uniform and stable items which are well understood, then the inputs are in quadrant 3. The increase which has taken place in the analysis of contracting situations over the past 20 years suggests that the construction industry has moved from quadrant 1 in the 1960s to quadrant 3 in the 1980s.

According to the theory the social technology, or the structure, should be in the same quadrant as the inputs. Figure 6.4 thus examines the social technology of the work unit. Again there are two dimensions. The horizontal dimension describes the extent to which the procedures which are applied to the inputs would be likely to

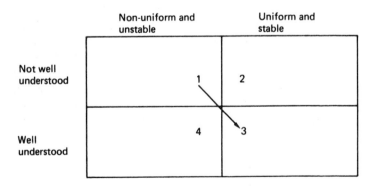

Figure 6.3 Perception and understanding of inputs to work units

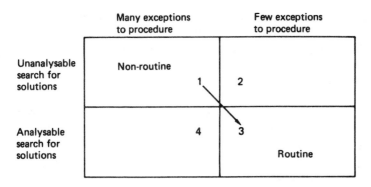

Figure 6.4 Social technology or procedure used to deal with input situations

contain exceptional, awkward pieces of information on a scale from few to many exceptions. The vertical dimension describes the process of enquiry which is triggered off when an exception occurs. Search procedures vary from being simple rules easily applied, to being complex sets of varying modes of searching between which judgements have to be made. The two dimensions are combined and related to the inputs so that the theoretically appropriate – and therefore most effective – social technology is located in the same quadrant as the inputs. This simple step in the analysis requires practice in its application, though this can be made simpler by the use of relatively straightforward research instruments. [15]

In practice, the framework can be used to evaluate the appropriateness of the designs of existing structures so that a lack of fit between inputs of information and social technology can be detected. The framework can also be used to identify the requirements for organisation redesign when it is known that existing patterns of inputs will be altered. For example, if the inputs to the work units handling tendering were to become more uniform and better understood, possibly as a consequence of improvements in 'expert systems' and in computer-based data sets, then the social technology of that work unit should be altered; similarly for on-site operations. If the informational inputs to some work units are becoming more unstable and are not well understood, then adjustments should be planned.

6.5.3 The firm and layers of decision making

The firm is a collection of work units which are differentiated from one another yet also integrated by various mechanisms. The work units are arranged in vertical layers of decision making as well as in different units within each lateral layer. One of the key questions concerns the relationship between the layers. How much autonomy do the layers have in their interrelationships with each other?

The social technology perspective can be used to explore this question by taking a simple illustration of changes which might occur in the structure of firms over a long period. On the assumption that the context of the construction firms has changed between 1965 and 1985 from one of highly variable inputs to more standardised inputs,[16] the theory would predict that the degree of autonomy of each level in its relationship to other levels in the successful, surviving, firms would be much tighter and more characterised by formalised procedures. The theory would also predict that the power of the lowest layer would be greatly reduced.

6.5.4 Technocrats and site managers

In an analysis of the firm, rather than of projects, the relationship between the technocrats at corporate headquarters and the site management is of key importance. The social technology perspective offers several important predictions.

Building on the early elements, it is possible to specify two dimensions: flexibility and centralisation. The theory predicts that the tasks of those in the operating layer (i.e., sites) can be used to prescribe the overall structure between technocrats and site management. Thus if the operating layer is characterised by stable, well understood inputs and has the appropriate social technology of highly analytic, straightforward search processes, then relations between site management and the techno-layer should be in the bottom left-hand quadrant of Figure 6.5. A possible long term movement in the relationships between the layers is from quadrant 1 to 3 to 4.

It now becomes possible to examine this relationship in more detail, taking three important indicators:

1. The extent to which work units possess *discretion* relative to others in the hierarchy.
2. The relative *power* of sub-units to influence other units above or below them in the hierarchy.
3. Whether *coordination within groups* (work unit levels) is based on rules and pre-planning or on continual mutual adjustment and feedback.

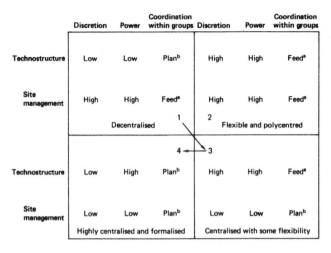

Figure 6.5 Types of decision making by technostructure and site management based on discretion, power and coordination within units

Note: *a* Feed – Continual mutual adjustment and feedback.

  b Plan – Risks and preplanning.

Source: Perrow, C.A., 'A Framework for the Comparative Analysis of Organisations', *American Sociological Review*, Vol. 32 (1967).

These three features are charted in Figure 6.5. As before, there are four quadrants. The basic principles may be illustrated by taking an example in which a firm moves from quadrant 1 to 3 over a long period of, say, two decades. At the start the firm would be in quadrant 1 and the technostructure would have low discretion and power and its internal coordination would be by simple planning. Its site management would possess high discretion and power, and achieve the internal site coordination by continual interaction and feedback. Later, these features are reversed as it moves to quadrant 3.

6.5.5 Top decisions and the environment

Clearly work units of top decision makers can be examined separately and in relation to the adjacent layer below them – the technostructure – as in the previous sections. However, top decision makers are also affected by external inputs to their decision making. Also the choices by top decision makers of the types of market segment to enter influence the type of contract which the firm has to process, and hence the operating level of the site.

The social technology perspective must therefore be applied to the external environment, such as illustrated in Sections 6.2 and 6.3 above, in order to assess whether there is a theoretically appropriate fit between that environment and the procedures used by top decision makers and by key technocrats. The external environment of the construction industry contains several distinct facets, each of which is the source of important informational inputs to the firm. The question is, to what extent are these inputs the source of high or low uncertainty in the informational structure and content?

All top decision makers will claim that there is high informational uncertainty about the future. However, within the social technology framework scales have been established to compare different sectors of the same industry and to make comparisons between industries. Clear differences have emerged in previous studies, therefore investigations of the external environment must be undertaken systematically.

There have been moves towards standardisation in the construction industry, particularly in the 1960s which saw the beginning of system building, and the prefabrication of components, the establishment of the *agrément* system and the creation of design packages. Many in the industry would argue that this trend has recently been reversed with more difficult sites leading to one-off buildings, even greater choice in materials and components and ever increasing variety in contractual arrangements. The important factor for the theory of social technology is not only – or even mainly – the variety and complexity of the inputs to construction, but the ability to order the information available so that the inputs to the decision making process can be more standardised. There may thus now be more information available in a better ordered manner about a greater variety of materials and components than previously when there were few materials and components but with too little information about them. In spite of the proliferation of materials and components, the decision maker may perceive his choice as being a simpler one now than hitherto, especially with the assistance of computer-aided design (CAD) and computer-aided management (CAM).

Indeed it is hypothesised that this is what has happened over the past 20 years or so in construction, say from 1966 to 1986. If so, there has been an increasing certainty in the inputs to top decision making. In this case, the whole structure of the firm should be either just inside the quadrant 3 in Figure 6.3, or at least close to the boundary line. Increases in certainty in the inputs surrounding the design of the contract may be accompanied by increasing competitiveness between firms.

6.6 INNOVATION, STRATEGIC POWER AND ORGANISATION LEARNING

Schumpeter[17] contended that capitalism was based on the introduction of routine procedures to achieve innovation in firms. That was an important observation because it highlighted the requirement for large firms to incorporate a capacity for transformational change within their multiple structures. In the study of industrial, military, health and educational enterprises there has been a growing pessimism about their capacity to sustain transformational change.[18] That pessimism contrasts with the optimism of the 1960s.

The degree of innovation by construction firms has not been systematically explored, but the social technology perspective offers several areas for investigation.

6.6.1 Innovation

Contemporary theories of innovation[19] distinguish two main types. First, most sectors and firms experience infrequent, relatively radical shifts in the product, in methods of construction and in forms of work organisation. These radical periods often consist of short, painful periods of transformation. Secondly, the radical transformation change is often followed by long periods of many years when there is more gradual, incremental innovation.

At one time it seemed that there was a life cycle for any sector and its constituent firms with respect to its requirements for social technology.[20] The assumption was that when a sector was founded, there were many small firms all handling non-uniform, unstable and confusing inputs which created exceptions that were difficult to analyse in a systematic manner. In other words, they were located in the top, left-hand quadrant (1) of our framework in Figure 6.3. Then, some firms discovered 'recipes' for satisfying customer demand and were able to increase their batch size and drive down costs so that rivals were eliminated. In this phase, the firms shifted out of the previous quadrant towards one of the other three quadrants, each of which is characterised by more incremental innovation. This model seemed to fit the automobile industry.[21]

The application of the life cycle model to the construction sector seems more problematic. However, the social technology approach can be used to examine the changing character of construction. If in fact the inputs to firms are becoming increasingly more ordered, and hence can be routinised, then consequent alterations should have been occurring in the structure. Given the competitive nature of the construction sector in the 1980s, it may be expected that those firms with inefficient structures will have been less profitable than others.

Where are innovation capacities located in the firm? The social technology perspective would suggest that the planning of future inputs is a key strategic area in the firm; often this activity is focused on the tendering processes. Given the previous assumptions, it is likely that in the past the tendering process became the focus of organisational efficiency and that the inputs of those units are now becoming increasingly routinised. It would follow from the theory that power accrues to those work units handling decisions of strategic importance.[22] It would also be expected that the whole firm would become more tightly bonded.

These observations raise an interesting point which lies outside the social technology framework. It is clear from comparative studies of British corporate management that in the manufacturing sector there has been a tendency to create a high degree of segmentation between the specialisms within the technostructure.[23] It is also clear that many firms outside construction are facing awkward problems of adjusting the managerial division of labour to remove barriers and to create more 'teamwork'. This is a crucial area because entrepreneurship stems from successful teamwork. The question is whether British construction firms have achieved the required change and, if so, does construction provide the model of innovation for the remainder of the British economy?

6.6.2 Organisation learning

Organisation learning is implied rather than dealt with directly by the social technology approach. The implication is that, as the inputs to work units and to firms as a whole vary, so it becomes necessary to alter what is being learnt. For example, if changes occur in the raw materials used by skilled craftsmen through the substitution of highly stable, preformed raw materials, then old skills become redundant and must be replaced by new, system oriented teamwork skills in order to achieve a tight efficiency in the operating system. The framework can thus be used to sketch the general type of skills which are required for the relationships between people and groups of people and to imply the sorts of personality characteristics (e.g., self-discipline) which ought to be engendered.

NOTES AND REFERENCES

1. The assumption is that structures vary in their capacity to carry information, and that different structures have specific cost characteristics. Thus, if the wrong structures are used, then either they will be insufficient for the task or they will be too expensive. Either way, the costs of information processing can be bettered by competitors. See Galbraith, J. R., *Organizational Design* (Wokingham: Addison Wesley, 1977) pp. 54ff.
2. Weber, M. (trans), *The Theory of Social and Economic Organisation* (New York: Free Press, 1947).
3. Pugh, D. S. and Hickson, D. J., *The Aston Programme, Volume I* (Aldershot: Saxon House, 1976).
4. Galbraith, J. K., *The New Industrial State* (London: Hamish Hamilton, 1967).
5. Galbraith, J. R., *Organizational Design* (Wokingham: Addison Wesley, 1977).
6. Organisation studies began by assuming a single structure; consequently the notion of dual structures seemed to be a paradigmatic leap forward. However, in order to cope with both incremental and radical innovations it has become clear that successful firms develop repertoires of (multiple) structures. That said, the refinement of the analysis of multiple structures is still in its infancy.
7. See the ESCR, WORC programme at Aston University, especially Whipp, R. and Clark P. A., *Innovation in the Automobile Industry: Product, Process and Work Organisation* (London: Frances Pinter, 1985).
8. The differentiation between work units in the same firm and the problems of integration are addressed very fully in Lawrence, P. R. and Lorsch, J., *Organisation and Environment: Matching Differentiation and Integration* (Cambridge, Mass.: Harvard University Press, 1967).
9. The politics of change was central to the seminal study by Burns, T and Stalker, G. M., *The Management of Innovation* (London: Tavistock, 1961). The problem of pre-existing and emerging political coalitions was largely sidelined until the publication of the best-selling book by Peters, T. J. and Waterman, R. H., *In Search of Excellence* (New York: Harper & Row, 1982). Even so, the analysis of political aspects is still relatively undeveloped and is awkward to incorporate into the essentially rational analytic models of the management sciences.
10. Whipp, R and Clark, P. A., 1985, *Innovation and the Automobile Industry: Product, Process and Work Organisation* (London: Frances Pinter, 1985).

11. There are two schools which have deeply influenced the study of structures and processes. The American Carnegie School included a prolific group of theorists including J. G. March, H. A. Simon, H. J. Leavitt, W. R. Dill, V. H. Vroom and R. M. Cyert in its first generation. The British group, known as the Aston Programme, included D. Pugh, D. J. Hickson, R. Hinings, T. Lupton, J. Child, D. Pheysey. Their studies are available in the series published by Saxon House (Aldershot) beginning with Pugh, D. S. and Hickson, D. J., *The Aston Programme, Volume I* (1976).

12. Reference to the seminal studies by Joan Woodward (1965, 1970) on structure and control systems, and by Burns and Stalker (1961) (see note 9) on routine, incremental innovation.

13. The social technology perspective as such was elaborated by C. A. Perrow in an over-concise and abstract article, 'A Framework for the Comparative Analysis of Organisations', *American Sociological Review*, Vol. 32 (1967) pp. 194–208, and later more fully explained in *Organisational Analysis: A Sociological View* (London: Tavistock, 1970). The framework has been used to examine several settings ranging from the kibbutz to libraries. More recently, R. L. Daft and N. B. MacIntosh undertook an interesting study of accountancy offices, (A Tentative Exploration into the Amount and Equivocality of Information Processing in Organisational Work Units', *Administrative Science Quarterly* (June 1981) pp. 207–24). There now exists a rudimentary and useful suite of research instruments for applying the scales.

14. This subfield, which was originally based on a relatively coherent set of basic postulates derived synthetically from several disciplines, had the potential to become codified by the mid-1970s when Jay R. Galbraith (see note 5) produced an excellent comprehensive treatment which could be used by firms in internal seminars. In effect, the possibility of an expert system seemed close. However, this potential was disrupted by the recognition that there were strong tendencies towards staticness and towards political conservatism. In the past ten years there has been the growth of a diversity of critiques from a more radical neo-Marxism perspective, most notably in critical theory. However, in the mid-1980s there was a return to the initial perspective and an attempt to revise it to cope with limitations.

15. Research instruments now exist for both descriptive studies by research analysts using observation and/or key respondents and for self-perceptions of information channels.

16. In a paper given to the Seventh Bartlett International Summer School (Lyons, France) the author used the social technology perspective in an analysis of a research study in British construction firms to identify changes occurring between 1965 and 1985. See Clark, P. A., 'The Economy of Time and the Managerial Division of Labour in the British Construction', BISS Proceedings, Vol. 7 (1985) pp. 130–43.

17. Schumpeter, J., *Capitalism, Socialism and Democracy* (New York: Harper & Row, 1942).

18. See especially Peters and Waterman (1982) (see note 9).

19. For a review of theories of innovation see Clark, P. A., *Anglo–American Patterns of Industrial and Commercial Innovation* (Berlin, New York: de Gruyter, 1987) Chapters 3–4.
20. Perrow, C. A., *Organisation Analysis: A Social View* (London: Tavistock, 1970) pp. 82ff.
21. Abernathy, W. J., *The Productivity Dilemma* (Baltimore: Johns Hopkins University Press, 1978).
22. See, for an up-to-date examination of the strategic contingencies theory of power, Hickson, D. J. *et al.*, *Top Decisions: Strategic Decision Making in Organisation* (Oxford: Basil Blackwell, 1985).
23. See the Anglo–German comparisons by J. Child and his colleagues.

Editors' Bridging Commentary

All previous chapters, explicitly or implicitly, have emphasised the importance of the quality of management. More than in many other industries, construction firms, with their low fixed capital assets, regard management as their scarce resource, particularly as the business of contracting is essentially the sale of management services. Contractors who fare badly or well may do so for a variety of reasons, many of which can be traced back to the quality of management.

Chapter 7 examines the behaviour of managers as individuals, the particular roles which they adopt, and the way in which they function and adapt to the organisation's structure.

The chapter also considers the appropriateness of various management structures and links with the analysis of organisations in Chapter 6. A number of practical questions raised by the concepts and ideas discussed in the chapter are drawn to the attention of decision makers.

7 Managers and the Organisation

Steven Male and Robert Stocks

7.1 INTRODUCTION

This chapter focuses on the individual manager within the organisation. First, it deals with what sort of person the manager is and what may be his own goals and aspirations; secondly, it looks at the roles of the manager in the firm; and thirdly, at some of the ways in which the manager functions. Clearly these aspects of managers and management are interrelated – for example, the sort of person the manager is will be one of the factors determining what he sees as his job and how he can carry out that job. However, for clarity they are dealt with separately. The relationship between the type of manager and structural features of the organisation is analysed in the last section.

7.2 MANAGERS AS INDIVIDUALS

7.2.1 Motivation

In order to understand how managers are likely to behave in given situations, it is necessary to consider their motivation.

One school of thought sees managers as responding to various needs – i.e., people have a variety of different needs which have a potential for determining behaviour. The needs for power, affiliation and achievement are among the most important in understanding organisational behaviour.

The need for power has been found to be the best predictor of managerial success, and it is therefore often regarded as the most important for those whose goal is to become managers or supervisors.[1] Indeed power and also conflict are seen as central features of organisational life. The need for affiliation is related to the desire to form interpersonal relationships; it is a particularly important motivational drive in group dynamics. Hunt[2] argues that 60 per cent of the workforce are more concerned with forming and maintaining

93

relationships rather than expressing the needs for power or achievement. Whereas the needs for power and achievement are more important at executive level, the fulfilment of affiliative or relationship needs therefore tends to dominate the thinking of people at the bottom of the organisational hierarchy. In the construction industry context, affiliative needs may be particularly important at site operative level. The need for achievement has been found to be characteristic of entrepreneurs.[3] Male,[4] in a wide ranging analysis of quantity surveyors, found them to be on average high need achievers. This could reflect the close linkage that quantity surveyors have with the economic operations of the construction industry. The need for power is closely related to the ability to exercise one of the functions of management, namely leadership. Wainer and Rubin[5] found that for the small company a high need for achievement and moderate need for power were related to high company performance. It was also found that the effects of the needs for power and affiliation on company performance operated through leadership style. A cautionary note is required, however, in that these results related specifically to small as opposed to large companies.

7.2.2 Factors in decision making

Generally, motivated behaviour is assumed to be intentional, voluntary and goal directed.[6] However, behavioural decision theories suggest that rationality cannot be assumed, and they provide an alternative description of an extension to the decision making process. In reality, managers make decisions based on implicit, intuitive and subjectively biased theories or models of organisations and people.[7] These factors are as likely to apply to managers of construction companies as to those in any other industry.

7.3 FUNCTIONS AND ROLES OF MANAGERS

7.3.1 Roles and strains

The behaviour and activities of an individual in a particular position are contained in the concept of role. Role theory is useful for conceptualising the manager in his interactions within the firm, and with the external environment. A role defines the expectations the individual has of himself and that others have of him when he occupies a given position in society or in the organisational system.[8] For example, within the context of a contracting firm the contracts manager acts as a link between the site and head office. The expectations of his behaviour and activities are structured within the two differing situations of site and head office.

Within the organisational system or group, the individual's values, beliefs and inclinations have a major influence on performance of his role. However, playing a particular role in time influences an individual's personality. An individual will inevitably have multiple roles. Role ambiguity results when there is some uncertainty in the mind either of the individual or of the membership of his role set, as to precisely what his role is at any given time.[9] Role overload occurs where the number of different roles which one person holds becomes too much for him; this is not the same as work overload. Role underload, on the other hand, results in a person believing he can cope with either a larger role or a greater number of roles than he presently fills.

Role stress takes two forms, either role pressure or role strain. The former is seen by Handy[10] to be beneficial stress whilst the latter is harmful stress. People need some stress to bring out the best in them, although too much can be harmful. A difficulty for the manager is knowing how much stress an individual can handle, and this is particularly relevant in construction especially at project level where it is difficult to gauge the site manager's ability to cope with larger or more complex situations.

7.3.2 Classification of functions and roles

There are several classifications of what managers do. A very useful one is that used by Mintzberg.[11] He contends that there are ten roles common to the work of all managers. These ten work roles are divided into three groups: interpersonnel, informational and decisional.

This classification can provide a useful basis for assessment of the nature of a job by weighing the importance of each role type. It can also be used for the assessment of managers by determining how well they perform in each role, hence evaluating their efficiency, and for matching the type of job with the type of manager. The likely activities in the construction industry context are discussed below.

The interpersonal roles

1. The *figurehead role* would include senior managers participating in the presentation of seminars, attendance at dinners, representing

the company on professional bodies. Other activities are also likely to include construction industry representation on government committees or pressure groups such as the Group of Eight and dealing with employee requests for occupational and other references.

2. The *leader role* includes virtually all activities concerned with subordinates and is the concern of executives, site managers, contracts managers, departmental heads. Because of its importance, it is discussed separately under *leadership* below.

3. The *liaison role* activities include contacts with clients and professionals at pre-tender stage, site visits by contracts managers, participating in site meetings, replying and dealing with suppliers, subcontractors.

The informational roles

1. The *monitor role* involves site visits, examination of technical press, newspapers, reports, site minutes, budget and finance reports, valuations, daywork sheets, departmental committees and board meetings.

2. The *disseminator role* involves providing information through company news sheets, internal memos, internal reports and site progress meetings.

   The monitoring and disseminating roles are closely linked. Senior managers of contracting companies constantly need to monitor and disseminate all available information towards strategic decision making.

3. The *spokesman role* is a public relations exercise which includes representation on trade associations. It includes the transmission of information to interested parties on company performance by meetings with stockbrokers and shareholders, annual reports, providing the press with information on, for example, contracts gained. The informational role of spokesman is very important and calls for effective presentation of the contractor's company image.

The decisional roles

The decisional roles are the most important aspect of the manager's work. They justify his authority and powerful access to information. Furthermore, they involve the manager in, and allow him to take full charge of, the strategy-making process of the organisation.

1. The *entrepreneurial role* is important in the corporate planning and innovation process. It involves the initiation of internal changes to the firm's structure. It requires action on company profit mark-ups on tenders. Other functions include takeover bids, mergers and divesting of company assets.

2. The *disturbance handler role* involves strategy or review sessions concerned with disturbances and crises facing the company. This may require action at international, national, local or site level. We can also expect responses to UK and overseas government policy which would be likely to have detrimental consequences for the firm. Examples include changes in interest rates and other political and economic action, the worsening of international diplomatic relations and the effects arising from the actions of competitors.

3. The *resource allocator role* is concerned with decisions on expansion into overseas markets and decisions on allocating resources towards corporate change, the allocation of head office and site staff to projects and committing resources to tendering. Resource allocation which implies the presence of integration also involves *control*. Control is concerned specifically with the extent to which differentiated activities are mutually supported and synchronised.[12] Anthony[13] is amongst those who view management control as the process by which managers ensure that resources are obtained and used effectively and efficiently to accomplish organisational objectives. The acquisition of information, the provision of feedback and measurement of job performance to increase motivation are amongst the prime reasons for control systems. Control requires measurement of performance and therefore records with information for the control system. Specific to the construction industry are:
   - progress control
   - labour demand charts
   - material control
   - plant and equipment control
   - cost control

4. The *negotiator role* is concerned with all aspects of labour negotiations at site, local, national and international level. It includes discussions with clients on contracts, negotiations with subcontractors and suppliers and with clients on contractual claims. This role may also involve participation in joint venture projects with other contractors.

The decisional roles are important at the strategic level since they involve planning and control. The resource allocator role is concerned with planning. Planning integrates the activities of the firm in order that it can effectively achieve its objectives.[14] Additional benefits include the reduction of uncertainty and improvement in communications. Poor quality of information and negative attitudes of individuals within the organisation are two potential major hindrances to planning.

Leadership

Though it is under the category of interpersonal roles, leadership is important throughout and needs to be considered separately. Theories developed in the 1960s show leadership as a function of the environment as much as of individual characteristics of leaders.

In a study of supervisor–subordinate relationships Likert[15] identified two basic types of leaders – namely autocratic or democratic – and defined them as either job or employee centred. Whilst taking the view that it is possible to derive generalisations or principles which are applicable to any situation, Likert saw four types of leadership style:

- Exploitative–authoritative
- Benevolent–authoritative
- Consultative system
- Participative group system.

Fiedler[16] adopts a contingency approach where there is seen to be no best way to suit every situation and an effective leader must match his style with the demands of a given situation. He provides three dimensions – namely, leader–member relations, task structure and positional power. The contracting company will face differing business situations which require differing styles of leadership. For example, at the policy level, in the interests of group cohesiveness, either a consultative or participative group system would be necessary. In a study of site based management Bresnan *et al.*,[17] have indicated that work is more task oriented, so that one of Likert's authoritative styles would be more effective. It should be stressed that both types of leader can be effective, depending upon the nature of the task and the characteristics of subordinates.

Fiedler has maintained that it is unrealistic to try and change an individual's leadership style because it is too deeprooted and stable and that it is more plausible to effect a change in situation by altering any of the three dimensions mentioned above. The leader is then able to develop a situation in which his style of leadership will be most effective. Fiedler appears to ignore the possibility that a leader may change his behaviour depending on the situation. For instance, while some leaders may think that it is somewhat of a luxury to take an interest in the workforce, others perceive that people will do a better job if one takes an interest in them. It is more likely that leaders in practice combine both these views as the situation requires.

It is important to remember that the board, or executive team, is the formal strategic decision making group in the company, and leadership style is only one important aspect. For the executive team to be effective, the group can be assumed to have the common interest of company survival. However, since each member of the board may represent different departments and interests within the firm, it is likely that they will bring to any board meeting different means to achieve this end.

7.4 RELATIONSHIP OF THE MANAGER TO THE STRUCTURE OF THE ORGANISATION

7.4.1 Hierarchical structures

Miles and Snow with others[18] have produced a strategic typology of organisations which reflects the relationship between managerial perceptions of the external environment, who the power holders are, and organisational politics on the one hand and the strategy, structure and process of organisations on the other hand. Since the executive team or board of directors will form the major decision making body of the contracting company, Miles and Snow's typology can, therefore, be used as a tool for examining managerial perceptions and decision making at this level.

It identifies four strategic company management types: defender, prospector, analyser and reactor. The defender company aims at stability and efficiency. It will tend to favour a formal hierarchical structure with extensive division of labour and strong central control. Information systems will be complex and vertical. Coordination mechanisms are likely to be simple and conflict will be resolved through hierarchical channels.

The prospector company will lay great stress on achieving flexibility by means of an informal and decentralised organisation with low division of labour. Information flows will tend to be horizontal and simple but there are likely to be complex mechanisms for coordination.

The analyser company comes somewhere in between the first two, aiming at the same time at stability and flexibility. The structure of the organisation will be loose with moderate central control. The coordination mechanisms will tend to be extremely complex and expensive. Conflicts will be resolved in many ways including hierarchical channels.

Lastly there is the reactor company which is unable to adopt a clean structure and will often show characteristics of the three previous types. Hence it is unstable. The organisation lacks a consistent set of response patterns to a changing environment.

Parsons[19] suggests there are three levels in the structure of any firm: the technical or production level, the organisational or managerial level and the institutional or community level. Kast and Rosenzweig[20] have adapted these into three hierarchical levels, interdependent systems that are present in any medium to large sized company. These systems are referred to as the technical system, the organisational level and the institutional level. The first, the technical system, is involved with the actual task performance of the organisation. For a contracting company this would be the site. Secondly, there is the organisational level which coordinates and integrates the task performance of the technical system and the institutional system. At this level, the primary function of management is the integration of people, information and material inputs to the technical and institutional levels. In the contracting company the buying, estimating and planning departments would be examples within the organisational level. The contracts manager would be an example of an integrator at the organisational level. Thirdly, the institutional level is concerned with relating and adapting the activities of the company to the business environment within which it operates. Kast and Rosenzweig argue that these three interdependent levels form the managerial system, span the entire organisation and integrate technology, people, resources and the company with the environment. However, since each level deals with different inputs, outputs and levels of uncertainty, managers will require a different orientation and sets of skills in order to deal with the requirements of their job.

A number of important points arise from this analysis for a construction company. At site level a manager (the technical manager) is task oriented; he is concerned with the technology required for construction; he will be using well known procedures and will have a short time horizon – the duration of the project. He will be involved in decisions based on facts and figures.

In the head office or regional office a manager (the organisational manager) is involved with a number of different projects, and he is primarily concerned with coordination. He has to be a political manager who is adept at compromise since he will have to balance the requirements of various departments and projects. He is involved with site level managers but has also to deal with senior managers. The organisational man has to deal with both short and long term time horizons. Since his decisions involve compromise he will require considerable interpersonal skills. This manager has to deal with the buying, planning, estimating and perhaps personnel departments as well as site agents, trade union representatives and senior managers involved in formulating company strategy.

The senior manager (the institutional manager) who deals with strategic decisions is constantly dealing with uncertainty. He requires conceptual skills and an ability to make decisions with only partial information. An example may be a decision to open a subsidiary regional office. The senior manager will have to make judgements on the political stability of a government, labour potential and likely competition. His time perspective is futuristic and long term. The implication for the large construction company is the ability either to train or hire managers that have the capability of adapting their skills from site level, through to middle management and finally into senior management where totally different orientations are required.

However, the picture described above is not so straightforward in practice. When considering the higher levels of the managerial hierarchy, the overall organisational structure of a firm will determine whether a manager will act in the capacity of either an organisational or institutional manager. An organisational structure can be viewed along a continuum of centralised to decentralised, that is according to the degree of decision making autonomy delegated to regional offices. A contracting company that retains much of the decision making power at head office can be said to be highly centralised. However, a company that gives decision making autonomy to the regions, with minimal head office interference, can be said to be decentralised. Consequently, the extent of centralisation–decentralisation will affect the activities of managers and subsequently their training for potential higher management posts within the overall company structure. For example, if a company has a regional structure which is highly centralised with little autonomy given to a regional office, then senior managers in the regional office will be representative of the organisational manager since they are really acting in a middle management capacity, primarily functioning as integrators. However, if a company decentralises decision making to the regional offices and regional autonomy is high, then senior regional managers may well be acting as institutional managers. In this instance, decentralisation of decision making means that regional managers will be concerned with adapting the regional organisation to the business environment and therefore require greater conceptual and judgemental skills. In addition, when senior regional managers are acting in the capacity of an institutional manager they are receiving the 'hands on' training and experience to equip them for senior executive positions at head office.

This approach links on to the structure of organisations using the social technology approach in Chapter 6. Here Clark uses four levels of the organisation in a contracting firm and discusses the interrelationships between the various levels.

7.4.2 Groups within the organisation

Groups form of their own accord within an organisation, but they can also be set up by managers. Groups can be utilised by managers to help in the decision making process and in the implementation of decisions. Group dynamics is concerned with internal relationships and with the external social environment;[21] groups are seen to be fundamental to the coordination of work in the organisation.[22]

The way groups operate depends very much on the people in it. The stronger the feeling of participation and belonging of its members, the stronger is the cohesiveness of the group. The levels of cohesiveness have some important consequences, such as improved performance, less staff turnover and absenteeism.

In a construction industry context, project team members who have worked together previously may be expected to be more cohesive because they have shared experiences. Additionally, the frequency with which the team meets is also important. Problems can, however, arise where there is little interpersonal attraction between group members and they do not share common interests, provide mutual satisfaction or pursue similar goals. Formal groups are more goal oriented and in an executive team situation, at the strategic level of decision making, group cohesiveness would be an important factor.

Formal meetings should, therefore, be encouraged, and decisions adhered to, and executive team members should participate in the decision making process. Leadership style becomes a further consideration in this respect. Group norms influence an individual's perceptions and the strength of a norm's influence depends positively on the group being highly cohesive. The norm should be highly relevant, and each member should understand the group criteria.

When dealing with complex problems, it has been shown that loosely structured groups have an initial advantage. However, tightly structured groups learn to communicate faster as they progress through the problem and their performance eventually becomes just as good as loosely structured groups.[23] Interpersonal conflict is always present to some extent in groups where members have different values, attitudes, beliefs and behaviour. A group develops its own unique culture and character as it becomes formalised and structured.

7.4.3 Managers and organisational politics

The political approach to organisations shows the pursuit of self-interests and power as the basic process in organisations. Political behaviour, in the organisational sense, is a claim by individuals or groups for organisational resources.[24] Change is always political, and occurs when a particular individual or group is able to impose its will on the organisational agenda.[25] Political action is likely to take the form of either manipulation or accommodation.

Handy,[26] in positing that all organisations are political systems, argues that most of the important decisions in organisations involve the allocation of, and competition for, scarce resources or influence. Individuals and interest groups differ in their opinions and values, preferences and beliefs, with a resultant conflict of priorities and goals. Power and conflict are seen as central features of organisational life. Overall strategies of political behaviour are seen by Newman *et al.*[27] to include the use of information, damaging the credibility of others, securing support through coalitions, and taking action at timely strategic moments. Mumford and Pettigrew[28] outline several factors which influence political behaviour, including the involvement of an expert or specialist, and uncertainty and risks associated with decisions. In an industry which contains many specialisms and much uncertainty and risk, a high level of political behaviour would be expected. For instance, large contracting companies are likely to have a number of central service departments whose interests may cut across organisational boundaries. A political manager will spend a good part of his time with outsiders on organisational politics. This will occur:

1. When the duties of his unit or department are so vague that no one can be sure of how effectively it is performing, for instance a personnel or training department.
2. When there is enough slack in the system to allow for such political activity – for example, when there is insufficient formal control in the company.
3. When the organisation's climate permits, perhaps when there are high levels of uncertainty and ambiguity in the firm concerning its goals and objectives.

These three situations can result from a lack of clarity and direction from board level.

7.5   IMPLICATIONS FOR THE FIRM

From the above discussion of various managerial concepts and theories it seems that the decision makers in contracting firms should pay particular attention to the following questions:

1. What the motivation of their personnel is, and the extent to which it might be regarded as appropriate and sufficient.
2. Whether the definition of roles is clear for each person, whether the sum of his roles is too substantial or too slight a load and whether the interrelationship of roles is sensible.
3. Whether the company's current system of job appraisal sufficiently utilises the evaluation of performance in roles as a facet of personnel appraisal.
4. Whether there is adequate training or other preparation for the assumption by individuals of new roles, including the membership of different groups.
5. What the leadership style or style appropriate to each function is, and how far the personnel employed in these functions match them, whether they are performing better in practice than the theory would suggest, and if so why.
6. Whether there are too many, or too few, formal groups or

suborganisations within the company; what the implications are for work load of senior managers and for decision making.
7. Whether the representation of particular functions on committees and groups correctly reflect their contribution to the company as a whole.

Some of the answers to these questions are suggested and discussed in the companion volume.

NOTES AND REFERENCES

1. See Feldman, D. C. and Arnold, H. J., *Managing Individual and Group Behaviour in Organisations* (Tokyo: McGraw-Hill, 1983) and Tichy, N. M., *Managing Strategic Change: Technical, Political and Cultural Dynamics* (New York: Wiley, 1983).
2. Hunt, J. W., *Managing People at Work* (London: McGraw-Hill, 1979) pp. 10–13.
3. McClelland, D. C., *The Achieving Society* (Princeton, N.J.: Van Nostrand, 1961).
4. Male, S. P., 'A Critical Investigation of Professionalism in Quantity Surveying', unpublished PhD, Heriot-Watt University (1984).
5. Wainer, H. A., and Rubin, I. M., 'Motivation of Research and Development Entrepreneurs', *Journal of Applied Psychology*, Vol. 53, No. 3 (1969) pp. 178–84.
6. Jung, J., *Understanding Human Motivation: A Cogitative Approach* (London: Collier Macmillan, 1978).
7. See Mintzberg H., *The Nature of Managerial Work* (New York: Harper & Row, 1973) and Tichy (1983) pp. 38–9 (see note 1).
8. Kast, F. E., and Rosenzweig, J. E., *Management and Organisation: A Contingency Approach*, 3rd edn (Tokyo: McGraw-Hill, 1979) p. 261.
9. Handy, C. B., *Understanding Organisations*, (Harmondsworth: Penguin, 1988).
10. Handy (1988) (see note 9).
11. Mintzberg (1973) (see note 7).
12. Child, J., 'Organisational Structure, Environment and Performance: The Role of Strategic Choice', *Sociology*, Vol. 6 (1972) pp. 1–22.
13. Anthony, P. D., *The Ideology of Work* (London: Tavistock, 1977).
14. Kast and Rosenzweig (1979) (see note 8) p. 70.
15. Likert, R., *New Patterns of Management* (New York: McGraw-Hill, 1961).
16. Fiedler, F. E., *A Theory of Leadership Effectiveness* (New York: McGraw-Hill, 1967).
17. Bresnan, M. J., Bryman, A. E., Ford, J. R., Beardsworth, A. D. and Keil, E. T., 'Leader Orientation of Construction Site Managers', *Journal*

of Construction Engineering and Management, Vol. 112 (September 1986) pp. 370–86.

18. Miles, R. E., Snow, C. C., Meyer, A. D. and Coleman, H. J. Jr, 'Organisational Strategy, Structure and Process', *Academy of Management Review* (July 1978) pp. 552, 554, 556. Also Robbins, S. P., *Organisational Theory: The Structure and Design of Organisation* (Englewood Cliffs, N.J.: Prentice-Hall, 1983) p. 103.

19. Parsons, T., *Structure and Process in Modern Societies* (New York: Free Press, 1960) pp. 60–96.

20. Kast, F. E. and Rosenzweig, J. E., 'The Modern View: a Systems Approach', in *Systems Behaviour*, 3rd edn, Open Systems Group (London: Harper & Row, 1981) pp. 52–6.

21. Melvin, T., *Practical Psychology in Construction Management* (New York: Van Nostrand, 1979) p. 182.

22. Mintzberg, H., *The Structuring of Organisations* (Englewood Cliffs, N.J.: Prentice-Hall, 1979) p. 106.

23. Carzo, R., 'Some Effects of Organisation Structure on Group Effectiveness', *Administration Science Quarterly*, Vol. 7 (1962–3) pp. 393–424.

24. See Bolman, L. G. and Deal, T. E., *Modern Approaches to Understanding and Managing Organisations* (London: Jossey-Bass, 1984) and Mumford, E. and Pettigrew, A. M., *Implementing Strategic Decisions* (London: Longman, 1975).

25. Bolman and Deal (1984) (see note 24).

26. Handy (1985) (see note 9).

27. Newman, W. H. *et al.*, *The Process of Management* (Englewood Cliffs, N.J.: Prentice-Hall, 1982).

28. Mumford and Pettigrew (1975) (see note 24).

Editors' Bridging Commentary

It is well-known that for over two decades there has been an increasing trend to replace directly employed labour in construction firms by subcontractors. Many contractors let work either to 'supply and fix' subcontractors, supplying both labour and materials, or to labour-only subcontractors. The variety of labour-only subcontractors is great, ranging from firms supplying labour on an agency basis, either on an hourly or daily basis, to gangs of men working together or single operatives with self-employed status.

The debate within and without the industry continues on the short and long term costs and benefits of labour-only subcontracting as opposed to direct employment including the long term problem of training. The present debate replaces an earlier one on casual employment of labour on sites. There has never been a large *permanent* directly employed labour force in the industry and this follows from the one-off, dispersed nature of building and civil engineering work.

Chapter 8, with its emphasis on efficiency criteria, shows that the theory has much to offer in the debate.

8 Manpower Management

Peter J. Buckley and Peter Enderwick

8.1 INTRODUCTION

Manpower management in the construction industry is heavily influenced by the particular characteristics of the industry described in the Introduction. The most significant include the substantial fluctuations in demand for construction, the labour intensive nature of much construction, employment instability, an unstable industrial structure which has been referred to as the 'construction jungle',[1] fragmented bargaining structures and the interdependence of trades as well as pervasive regulation. Analysis is also complicated by the diversity of labour management practices. Within private construction unionised trades and firms coexist with a significant non-union sector and a large casualised subcontracting industry. The emphasis in this chapter is on private sector construction and particular attention is paid to the growth of 'labour-only' subcontracting.

The benefits of an examination of manpower management within construction are considerable. Firstly, the industry provides an interesting case study for the testing of recent ideas on employment contracts and the development of internal labour markets which highlight the fixity of labour. These concepts, which have been widely applied to manufacturing, may require modification in view of the nature of the construction industry. Secondly, our discussion may yield useful lessons for the practical management of labour. Thirdly, labour management in the construction industry impinges on a number of areas of public policy. Perhaps the most pressing are the social costs of employment instability and the depressingly high rates of work-related deaths and accidents in construction. Finally, manpower practices in construction are likely to be highly 'visible' and a source of influence on other sectors of the economy. This visibility follows from the geographical dispersion of construction activity and the extensive interindustry movement of workers with core skills widely used in construction.

There is a large established body of theory dealing with manpower in industry, and in the 1970s it was developed considerably to utilise jointly the ideas of management and economics. Three areas are selected here:

1. Arrangements for the use of labour, particularly the labour or employment contract and the internal labour market
2. Control of the operations of labour, notably the hierarchical system
3. Measures of efficiency of the system

Some theoretical ideas relating to each of these will be discussed and then their relevance to the construction industry will be considered.

8.2 THE ECONOMICS OF WORK ORGANISATION

Economic analysis of the organisation of work has been hampered by the traditional orientation of the theory of the firm as an element in the neoclassical determination of relative prices (see chapter 9). Attention was focused not on how firms behave but rather on how, in aggregate, they respond to changes in environmental factors. Implicit within this view of the firm was the existence of fully specified production functions operating at, or close to, optimum efficiency. The effects of this were to exclude the need for any consideration of why firms exist, how they are likely to be organised, and how inputs are managed.

8.2.1 The employment contract and the internal labour market

Recent work deriving from a seminal article by Coase (1937)[2] (Buckley and Casson, 1976; 1985; Leibenstein, 1976; Williamson, 1975; 1980)[3] which takes contractual exchange as the central element of economic activity, opens up a richer vein for the examination of manpower management. Contracts for labour services highlight the essential problems of economic exchange and illustrate the viability of alternative contracting forms. Contracts are diverse and often incomplete. They cover not only the price and utilisation of labour inputs but also the rights of both the individual concerned and the position of relevant parties to the agreement such as unions and management. Additional terms may specify institutional arrangements for administration, interpretation and enforcement of the agreement. Contractual incompleteness follows from requirements of flexibility. In the face of uncertainty, adaptability in the definition of tasks and responsibilities is essential.

A variety of alternative contractual forms with different degrees of flexibility can be invoked. The simplest is a basic sales contract whereby the parties contract for a predefined performance at a future date. However, the rigidity of simple sales contracts restricts their applicability under conditions of complexity and uncertainty, as is generally the case with the employment of labour. A second form is a contingent claims contract where a future outcome is contingent on the occurrence of some previously defined event. The considerable problems involved in drawing up contingent claims contracts are a limiting factor in their use. Additional problems occur in defining and obtaining mutual agreement on the occurrence of particular events. Thirdly, a series of the sales contracts can be negotiated over time as performance dictates. Sequential contracting involves high negotiation costs and ignores worker heterogeneity and the desire of employers to retain certain types of labour. This desire is reflected in the development of arrangements to curb labour turnover. The fourth contractual mode is the authority relationship as developed by Simon,[4] whereby one party (the employee) allows the other (the employer) to select the required performance from within a previously defined and agreed range. Labour enjoys income and employment stability at the price of giving up control over the labour process. Flexibility is obtained at the cost of vagueness. Renegotiation difficulties emerge when events compel the selection of a performance level from outside the implicit (or explicit) range previously agreed.

This focus on contracting or transaction costs (see Chapter 1) provides insights into the existence, size and structure of firms. Coase,[5] argues that firms exist because they enable exchange to be achieved at lower cost when it is internalised (i.e., taken out of external markets). The economies of internalisation stem from transaction cost savings. Internalisation results in savings in costs of acquiring information, particularly of relevant prices, as well as substituting an employment relationship for a series of former complete (external) contracts. A major omission of this analysis is its lack of specification of the typical organisational structure of firms – that is, why the employment relation is hierarchically structured.

8.2.2 Structure of organisations and the labour market

Explanations of hierarchical employment relationships have focused on two primary reasons. The first is the efficiency benefits which derive from hierarchical organisation. The second is the control function of hierarchical structure, particularly its effects in reducing the bargaining power of labour. It is useful to invoke the distinction which McPherson[6] makes between vertical and horizontal hierarchy. Vertical hierarchy refers to the fact that ultimate control in business organisations lies with the owners and their management representatives. Horizontal hierarchy relates to the arrangements which result in the differentiation of employees in terms of grades, ranks and rewards.

An influential efficiency oriented explanation of hierarchical organisation is that of Alchian and Demsetz,[7] who perceive such structures as a response to the labour management problem. The problem is the need to both monitor and reward effort where team production makes it difficult to evaluate the output contribution of individual team members. Hierarchical organisation facilitates this monitoring process. In addition, to minimise the need to monitor 'monitors', motivational incentives can be provided by which monitors become residual claimants on the enterprise's income. Such a distinction in both size and source of income represents a basis for the vertical hierarchical ordering of employees. This analysis of a simple firm can be readily extended to cover the larger management controlled enterprise.[8]

Williamson[9] has developed this line of reasoning to account for the horizontal hierarchy apparent within larger employing units. Here the monitoring of effort by a sole proprietor or the replication of successive supervisory levels is subject to the rapid onset of diminishing returns. Furthermore, Williamson's treatment focuses on tasks which are non-homogeneous. Non-homogeneous tasks involve high costs of management time as transactions are negotiated and executed. These problems are exacerbated in complex and uncertain situations where decision makers are subject to bounded rationality, where information and the capacity to analyse it is limited, and there is the possibility of opportunistic behaviour where information is unevenly distributed. The variation between individuals in the capacity to analyse situations cannot be costlessly reduced and provides a source of bargaining power. Opportunistic behaviour extends the concept of self-interest to encompass the use of guile. Such behaviour arises primarily from partial or distorted information disclosure and misrepresentation of intentions.

The modern corporation has gone beyond the simple authority relationship in an attempt to overcome these limitations. The emergent form is the employment relationship within an internal labour market (ILM).[10] An ILM exists when the allocation and pricing of labour occurs primarily within the organisation and incumbents are differentiated from labour in the external market. Such an arrangement offers a number of potential advantages. When individual contracts are replaced by a general collective agreement, the rigidity of the authority relationship is reduced. Furthermore, peer group involvement increases the likelihood of a constructive response to change. The substitution of a collective agreement for a series of individual contracts stresses the importance of organisational interests over individual concerns and reduces the incentives for opportunistic behaviour. The assignment of wage rates to tasks as opposed to individuals serves to increase flexibility.

The incentive group structure of the ILM facilitates efficient internal exchange. A promotional–reward system based on seniority fosters cooperation and the sharing of task-specific knowledge. Screening can be achieved at a lower cost and risks can be reduced when entry to the group occurs mainly at lower level positions. Such an arrangement also discourages labour turnover since the loss of seniority and other pecuniary rights are a disincentive to mobility. The system is strengthened when self-monitoring of groups is encouraged and internal methods of conflict resolution are set up.

In a critique of this efficiency oriented theory a number of researchers have offered a very different explanation for the emergence of centralised hierarchical production.[11] These writers argue that whilst hierarchical and centralised organisation are not unique to the capitalist mode of production, its features under capitalism are distinct. The extensive division of labour is thought to stem not only from technical superiority but from a need for the entrepreneur to ensure for himself an essential role in the productive process. With the increasing separation and specialisation of tasks and a restriction of the area of market based decision making, the need for an integrating intermediary arises. Similarly, hierarchical and centralised organisation of production enables a substitution of the employer's preferences on labour utilisation and capital accumulation for those of his employees. This vertical hierarchy is complemented by horizontal segmentation whereby employers enjoy advantages from dividing a potentially cohesive labour force.[12]

This critique raises three important issues. First, where wage and non-wage conditions are set by joint employer–employee bargaining, management may be tempted to develop organisational structures oriented to goals other than output efficiency. If the relative bargaining power of labour depends on its cohesiveness, which in turn is partly dependent on organisation structure and management strategy, then organisational design may be based on both productive efficiency and labour control considerations. In brief, management concern will focus on both the distribution of the firm's product as well as the size of that product.[13] Second, if one accepts the argument that labour effort should be seen as a variable productive input, the concept of output efficiency is thrown into question. Since the expected labour input is poorly defined (i.e., incomplete contracts) closer supervision of labour (number of workers) may raise output but only by increasing the input (effort level) of those units. Third, it is apparent that the opportunity for adopting a productively inefficient but control enhancing organisational structure depends on the existence of market imperfections. In the absence of imperfections workers would be tempted away by more productive competitors (or labour managed firms) offering higher returns. In the case of the labour market such imperfections are all too prevalent.

8.2.3 Efficiency criteria

A number of criteria for judging the relative efficiency of alternative modes of work organisation may now be established. Williamson[14] presents three groups of efficiency indicators:

– Attributes relating to the flow of products
– The efficiency of employee task assignment
– Incentive properties

1. *Product flow indicators* refer to the costs of transferring work-in-progress between work stations – that is, the point at which production or processes are undertaken – the costs of maintaining buffer inventories between stations, and product losses at successive processing stages. Modes of organising tasks which minimise transfer, inventory and leakage costs will be preferred.
2. *Efficient task assignment* requires that individuals be allocated to those tasks where they enjoy comparative advantage – that is, where they are relatively better at doing the job than others – that

there should be effective coordination of tasks and the exercise of effective leadership, and that there should be appropriate contracting with service specialists. Preferred modes will ensure efficient assignment to tasks, economise on coordination costs and allow effective contracting with specialist functions.

3. *The incentive attributes* of alternative modes are judged on the basis of whether they produce high work intensity, efficient utilisation of equipment, the adoption of cost saving innovations and the development of adaptability and responsiveness.

8.3 THE CONSTRUCTION INDUSTRY AND THE THEORY

8.3.1 Introduction

It can be seen from Section 8.2 above that theory would suggest that internal labour markets would be the most efficient method of operation. In construction, however, there has been a movement, at least since the beginning of the 1960s,[15] towards less, rather than more, internalisation of the labour market. In the UK between 1965 and 1982 the number of construction workers operating under labour-only contracts rose from around 160 000 to 200 000 to a possible 600 000.[16] In 1977 labour-only subcontracting firms accounted for 24 per cent of the training levy collected by the CITB. By 1982 they provided about 43 per cent.

The theory would thus seem to need adjustment as an explanation of the situation in the construction industry. The source of the adjustment will be looked for in the characteristics of the industry as a whole. The reasons why individual firms use labour-only subcontracting are of course part of the field work described in the companion volume.

8.3.2 Characteristics of the construction industry

The defining features of the construction industry include product customisation, a fragmented industrial structure and sensitivity to cyclical fluctuations in output and employment. Product customisation follows from the nature of demand facing the industry. Demand, while geographically dispersed, cannot generally be met by centralised production; output tends to be locationally-specific. Customisation is also encouraged by the existence of scale economies in the finished product.[17]

The fragmentary industrial structure of the construction industry is the result of a number of economic factors. The pattern of demand with a large number of small value orders, the extensive division of labour and specialisation of skills, ease of entry, particularly into the specialist trades, minimal vertical integration and limited opportunities for the achievement of absolute cost advantages through large scale activity are all consistent with a fragmented economic structure. There is also evidence of decreasing mean size measured in terms of numbers employed but not in terms of turnover, which is compatible with the growth of labour-only subcontracting. This development is also compatible with the large number of very small specialist trade firms found in the construction industry. However, large firms are still growing larger in turnover terms, even after allowing for inflation. Absolute firm size is favoured by technological developments such as the introduction of reinforced concrete[18] or the implementation of building codes and standards.[19]

8.3.3 The effects of fluctuations

Fluctuations in overall demand, and hence in output, are substantial in contracting and when output for a particular type of work in a specific geographical area is considered, the fluctuations may be very wide indeed. The first consequence of these output fluctuations is a preference for short term contracting.[20] Management will seek, wherever possible, to obtain factor services on short duration contracts (e.g., plant hire). The labour intensity of construction means that this preference will be particularly strong in the case of labour. The widespread use of selective tendering for projects or parts of a project accentuate instability and encourage specialisation in subcontracting.[21]

Secondly the characteristics of construction are not conducive to the development of employment relations governed by an internal labour market. The insulation of employees from the vagaries of demand assumes that to some extent such variability can be managed or regulated by the organisation. While ILMs offer a degree of flexibility[22] they are unlikely to be able to cope with the marked fluctuations experienced within construction. A more likely response is the shifting of risk to labour in the forms of self-employment and dependent subcontracting.[23] This strategy is particularly attractive when there exist financial and other advantages of self-employment.[24]

Thirdly, internalisation of the labour market is further discouraged by the slow rate of technical progress within construction, and the continued dominance of handicraft labour which has limited management attempts to control the labour process. Where work is not machine paced and regulated the returns to traditional skills of organising tasks and maintaining quality remain high.[25]

8.3.4 The effect of the unions

The UK evidence

Unions actions affect not only the actual conditions of the labour contract but also the attitude of employers.

Union organisation is generally low in construction, though it is more fully developed for craftsmen. One estimate is that around 1982–3 only 40–50 per cent of directly employed operatives were members of a union; the proportion of craftsmen may have been as high as 75 per cent. However, if the total of directly employed and self-employed operatives are taken together the proportion who were members of a union is less than 30 per cent.[26] This is not inconsistent with earlier estimates. The work of Bain[27] suggests an overall union density rate for construction in 1979 of 36.7 per cent; this is considerably below the manufacturing industry average of 69.8 per cent. Union density in construction declined by nearly 10 percentage points from 1948 to 1979.[28] Official estimates suggest a further decline since 1981.[29] These low levels of union organisation are to be expected in an industry typified by small size employing units, intermittent work opportunities and high labour turnover.[30]

However, in spite of this low density of union membership, the constraints imposed by the unions on contractors may well have been instrumental in pushing employers away from the internal labour contract which is easily monitored by unions to the external labour contract of labour-only subcontracting.

Despite the low overall level of unionisation in construction there is considerable reliance on closed shop agreements, particularly for craft occupations. At the beginning of the 1960s some 100 000 construction employees (about 6 per cent of the labour force at that time in the UK) were subject to such agreements.[31] In 1978 a minimum of 7 per cent of employees were in a closed shop situation and an interesting feature of such agreements in construction is their informality (i.e., they are not covered by a written agreement).[32]

The incidence of strikes can be a disruptive feature. A study of

Britain in 1970–5 revealed that construction consistently suffered more strikes per 100 000 employees in each of the years 1970–5, and the average for those years was some 50 per cent above the median for all industries and services.[33] However, the number of days lost per 1 000 persons employed was consistently lower than in all industries and services, with the dramatic exceptions of 1972 when it was over three times as many. Hillebrandt found that the number of working days lost per 1 000 persons in employment were few and less than in industry as a whole in most years.[34] In 1987, the total days lost in construction was at a long term low of 19 000 out of 525 000 in all industries, or a mere 0.5 per cent of the total.[35]

In the longer run, union opposition may have inhibited the rate of technological progress in construction. From the period after the Second World War the craft based nature of many construction unions led to attempts to organise and control changes in the work process resulting from technological advance.[36]

In the UK, the construction unions have not succeeded in pushing up earnings to those of other industries. Recorded average gross weekly earnings in construction in each year from 1976 to 1986 were lower than in all industries and services, but in the boom period of the early 1970s they were actually higher.[37] However, the wages negotiated by the unions are considerably lower than the rates actually paid. It is interesting that the UK is near the bottom of the league of developed countries, having substantially lower earnings in construction than in manufacturing. Indeed in many higher income countries construction earnings in 1986 were higher than in manufacturing, notably in the USA, Sweden, Denmark, Norway, Australia, Japan, Finland and the USSR, whereas most developing countries had lower earnings in construction than in manufacturing.[38]

However, in spite of the UK wage situation, there is no doubt that the non-wage factors attributable to the unions militate against the internal labour market.

The US evidence

The situation in the USA is different from that in the UK in many respects. First, in the USA there is considerable evidence that construction is a relatively high wage sector.[39]

In the mid-1970s average hourly construction earnings in the USA exceeded the manufacturing average by nearly 50 per cent. A positive differential is to be expected for a number of reasons. First, the high proportion of skilled manuals tends to inflate the industry average. Second, the underprovision of wage supplements in construction may be partially offset by high wage rates. Third, employment instability means that generous hourly rates do not necessarily translate into high annual earnings. Evidence indicates that in 1969 only 60 per cent of all construction employees worked full time. As a result, median annual earnings in construction tend to be below those in manufacturing.[40] Foster[41] suggests that less than half of the favourable differential enjoyed by construction can be attributed to skill differences and the low level of fringe benefits. This suggests either a significant element of compensation for the unfavourable traits of construction employment (high levels of risk, employment instability, etc.) or the existence of a sizeable union impact.

There is additional evidence which tends to favour the latter hypothesis. First, direct tests of the non-wage union effect in construction suggest a discernible if not very sizeable impact. Mandelstamm[42] found that the higher wage costs of unionised building workers in Michigan were offset by a comparable productivity differential. More recent studies, particularly by Allen, confirm the union productivity differential which appears to be significantly higher than that typical of manufacturing. Accounting for the difference has proved more difficult, with some tentative evidence of fewer resources devoted to supervision in the union sector and incentives to a greater use of standardising components resulting from higher union wage rates.

Second, Haber and Levinson[43] found evidence of the existence of 'featherbedding' and some restrictions on piecework. They estimated that the total effect of union job regulation added between 3 and 8 per cent to the cost of a completed house.

Lastly, other evidence of the strong influence of unions comes from the prevalence of closed shop agreements,[44] leapfrogging in wage agreements because of the many unions[45] and the high incidence of disputes.[46]

Government pressure for a reform of bargaining structures has existed for a number of years in the USA. There is evidence of a gradual widening of units, particularly on a geographical basis, since benefits in the form of reduced strike action, an elimination of 'leapfrogging' and enhanced competitiveness of the union sector *vis-à-vis* the non-union sector accrue to union officials, contractors and construction users.

All this in spite of the fact that the level of unionisation in construction was estimated at about 55 per cent for craftsman and

30 per cent for labourers.[47] However, it must be remembered that there is a great diversity of conditions in this respect in the USA and that the union structure is quite different from that in the UK.

8.3.5 Control of the labour input

The hierarchical structure, control and efficiency mechanism presented above in Section 8.2.2 is more relevant to the internal labour market than to subcontracting. However, this does not mean that it is not relevant to the employment of management teams, which are stable and internalised in large parts of the construction industry.

Moreover, the benefits of subcontracting may well encompass control attributes. While management has never been able fully to control the craft based work process in construction, their influence may be enhanced where subcontracting is prevalent. Firstly, such a mode creates dual dependence: the worker depends on the subcontractor for his wage while employment opportunities are the domain of the principal contractor. Secondly, the system proved efficient in responding to labour shortages in the 1960s. Subcontracting allowed earnings to be bid up when demand required but such increases were never consolidated through collective bargaining. Thirdly, the opportunities for increased earnings discouraged reliance on construction unions and fostered self-employment. Fourthly, subcontracting strengthened both horizontal and vertical hierarchy of workers, causing divisions within the workforce. The coexistence of workers employed by different firms, under different terms and arrangements and for varying durations weakens labour cohesion and the identification of mutual interest.[48]

8.3.6 Efficiency criteria

In terms of the efficiency criteria set out in Section 8.2.3, subcontracting offers a number of benefits. Some form of continuous contracting is likely to be preferred under the conditions of uncertainty widespread in construction. Subcontracting arrangements have good assignment attributes but, when operated in manufacturing, are weak in terms of product flow and incentive attributes.[49] Significantly, when applied to construction many of these weaknesses are attenuated.

Subcontracting is an efficient system for ensuring assignment of individuals to tasks: the assignment problem is assumed by a main contractor or individual subcontractor both of whom are likely to be better informed about the attributes of potential workers or teams than the principal. Furthermore, the fuller utilisation of teams through subcontracting ensures the development and maintenance of comparative advantage in tasks. The issue of leadership is also resolved in a low cost way through subcontracting. Discriminatory leadership follows where subcontracting teams are led by a master or rewarded on a lump sum basis. Subcontracting does make extensive demands on management expertise in coordination, but these are just the sorts of qualities which are very important (if not often recognised) in the construction industry.[50] Similarly, the form of projects with the progressive embodiment of specialist contributions are amenable to systematic planning and coordination. Subcontracting also allows the efficient integration of non-operating specialists (e.g., inspectors) by pre-scheduling and discrete completion. Subcontracting appears then to be efficient in terms of assignment attributes.

More doubt attaches to its efficiency benefits with respect to product flow and incentive attributes. Product flow questions of transportation and buffer inventory costs are of lesser significance in construction compared to manufacturing. The centralisation of production and of inputs serves to minimise transport costs between work stages.

The careful planning and coordination of projects means that buffer inventories are not really applicable; rather, reliable start and completion times for tasks are more important. Information regarding the performance of subcontractors with respect to these criteria is collected more efficiently by operations management and main contractors; multi-site operations offer opportunities for the pooling and updating of such information. More important in construction is the need to minimise interface leakage which may occur through theft or a reduction in quality of intermediate products. Labour-only subcontracting allows the principal contractor control over input (materials, plant, etc.) quality but at the price of assuming wastage costs. Where activities are performed on-site the monitoring of performance or metering of inputs can be achieved at relatively low cost.

Incentive attributes cover work intensity, equipment utilisation, innovation and adaptability. Subcontracting is efficient in ensuring high work intensity. When quality is unimportant or easily monitored, subcontractors may be remunerated on a piece-rate system. There is also some tentative evidence[51] that the use of Payment by

Results (PBR) is particularly widespread in crafts such as plastering and carpentry, where quality is easily observed. In addition, these are not processes likely to generate cost or safety externalities when quality is shaded because of piece-work incentives.

Equipment misutilisation risks in construction can be minimised in two principal ways. First, major plant can be hired, thus ensuring that depreciation costs remain with the owner. Second, the probability of misutilisation can be further reduced by hiring both equipment and operator, who presumably has incentives to ensure its efficient use. Unlike manufacturing much capital in construction takes the form of handtools which are owned and provided by individuals employed under subcontract. Innovation incentives are strong under subcontracting where individuals are able to appropriate for themselves the fruits of innovation.

Subcontracting is weak in terms of ensuring cooperative behaviour and adaptation to change. Exact contractual responsibilities assumed by the different parties are a constant source of divisiveness since they are a major determinant of profitability. Subcontractors face no incentives to cooperate in adapting to changing circumstances, particularly if such adaptation increases their work load. This problem is particularly evident when tasks are remunerated on a lump sum basis.

8.3.7 The social costs of subcontracting

The above discussion focused on private efficiency benefits. It is possible that subcontracting may generate negative externalities, thus raising social costs, and these may be industry costs or national costs. One area where this is particularly likely is safety. The system of subcontracting clouds the division of responsibilities over aspects of health and safety. This is of some significance in the UK where reliance is placed on a self-regulating system.[52] In the USA, it has been estimated that the total cost (the sum of social and private costs) of an accident is five times the private cost.[53]

Another cost of subcontracting, initially external to the firm, is that of training. There are great problems in getting labour-only subcontractors to undertake training and the established system of training by apprenticeship in the construction industry has been seriously eroded by the growth of subcontracting.

These issues all imply that manpower management in construction is an important policy matter.

8.4 MANPOWER MANAGEMENT IN THE INTERNATIONAL CONSTRUCTION INDUSTRY

When we turn to the question of manpower management in the international construction industry, the focus of attention is broadened to include both direct and indirect labour. The prevailing paradigm within international business theory highlights the interaction of a number of interrelated factors.[54] The growth of the international contractor arises from the benefits of internalising markets across national boundaries. In this way, the contractor can combine his firm-specific assets with the location-specific factors to be found in foreign countries. In international construction, management provides a crucial source of firm-specific asset. As Casson[55] has argued, the existence of multi-locational enterprises of indefinite life results from the possession of knowledge that is both general and durable. Such knowledge is embodied in the managerial employees of the enterprise.

An important knowledge based asset of contracting firms is the ability to coordinate and manage projects. In contrast to manufacturing, construction places a premium on skills of managing by continual intervention.[56] Similarly, the importance of pre-qualification processes in international tendering suggests that the assimilation and maintenance of expertise in this area may constitute a major competitive weapon. Empirical evidence shows that tendering costs for overseas projects are some one to two times as great as those of domestic projects of the same size. Evaluation of initial tenders places primary importance on previous experience in work of a similar type.[57] These findings suggest the existence of both barriers to new entrants (i.e., advantages enjoyed by incumbent firms) and economies of maintaining corporate teams.

These labour based advantages of contractors may be reinforced by source country-specific factors. It has been suggested that British construction firms may benefit from the international experience and reputation of related professions such as consultant engineers, architects and surveyors.[58] Similarly, construction firms based in the developing economies have achieved notable success in obtaining overseas contracts, particularly within other developing nations.[59] Their access to low cost labour, experience of working to Third World standards, willingness to exploit appropriate (labour intensive) production functions and ability to manage developing country workforces are important competitive elements. The success of South Korean firms in the Middle East market is a good example. In 1982, over 70 per cent of developing country projects undertaken by South Korean firms were in the Middle East. These firms had more than 61 000 Korean workers deployed in the Middle East in the mid-1970s.[60] The barriers to the use of imported labour which exist in most advanced economies are consistent with the failure of Third World construction firms to penetrate these markets.[61]

Internationalisation also works to reinforce firm-specific advantages. Overseas involvement provides one form of diversification, and if counter-cyclical will contribute to the maintenance and fuller utilisation of team knowledge. Furthermore, the international arbitrage of overseas experience in several markets may offer synergistic economies. Similar benefits can be obtained from involvement in overseas consortia whereby participants gain from the complementarity of inputs, the spreading of risk and immediate access to local market knowledge. The labour based nature of firm-specific advantages are also consistent with the widespread use overseas of management contracts.[62]

Interestingly, the limited empirical work on international contracting suggests that consideration such as the domestic underemployment of resources, the maintenance of specialist teams or experience of overseas operations are not primary motives for internationalisation. Rather, firms report a desire to expand when domestic growth is constrained or where shareholders interests benefit from diversified operations.[63] This is clearly an area where more empirical investigation is warranted.

8.5 CONCLUSIONS

This chapter has applied a contractual approach to the management of labour in the construction industry. It is found that the special characteristics of construction – notably fluctuations and uncertainty – mean that, unlike the situation in manufacturing industry, subcontracting offers a low cost mode of organising work in the construction industry, and this is borne out by the discussions with contractors reported in the companion volume. The weaknesses of subcontracting in manufacturing in terms of product flow and incentives are attenuated in the construction industry, and there are great advantages in the assignment of individuals to tasks.

Labour-only subcontracting offers advantages in efficiency and in control. The private advantages of labour-only subcontracting have to be tempered by the social costs of failure to train and a possible reduction in safety.

It is, by contrast, to the advantage of the contractor to maintain his managers, a very important asset to any firm, internal to the firm and here the internal labour market is the norm. This is clear particularly from a consideration of the overseas contracting market.

NOTES AND REFERENCES

1. Stallworthy, E. A. and Kharbanda, O. P., *International Construction and the Role of Project Management* (Aldershot: Gower, 1985).
2. Coase, M., 'The nature of the firm', *Economica*, Vol. 4 (1937) pp. 386–405.
3. Buckley, P. J. and Casson, M., *The Future of the Multinational Enterprise* (London: Macmillan, 1976), Buckley, P. J. and Casson, M., *The Economic Theory of the Multinational Enterprise* (London: Macmillan, 1985), Leibenstein, H., *Beyond Economic Man* (Cambridge, Mass.: Harvard University Press, 1976), Williamson, O. E., *Markets and Hierarchies, Analysis and Anti-Trust Implications* (New York: Free Press, 1975), and Williamson, O. E., 'The organisation of work: a comparative institutional assessment', *Journal of Economic Behaviour and Organisation*, Vol. 1 (1980) pp. 5–38.
4. Simon, H. A., *Models of Man* (New York: Wiley, 1957).
5. Coase, M. (1937) (see note 2).
6. McPherson, M., 'Efficiency and Liberty in the Productive Enterprise: Recent work in the economics of work organisation', *Philosophy and Public Affairs*, Vol. 12 (1983) pp. 354–68.
7. Alchian, A. A. and Demsetz, H., 'Production, information costs and economic organisation', *American Economic Review*, Vol. 62 (1972) pp. 777–95.
8. Jensen, M. C. and Meckling, W. H., 'Theory of the firm: managerial behaviour, agency costs and ownership structure', *Journal of Financial Economics*, Vol. 3 (1976) pp. 305–60.
9. Williamson (1975) (see note 3).
10. Doeringer, P. and Piore, M., *Internal Labor Markets and Manpower Analysis* (Lexington: D. C. Heath, 1971) and Osterman, P. (ed.), *Internal Labor Markets* (Cambridge, Mass.: MIT Press, 1984).
11. See Edwards, R., *Contested Terrain: The Transformation of the Workplace in the Twentieth Century* (London: Heinemann, 1979).
12. Gordon, D. M., Edwards, R. and Reich, M., *Segmented Work, Divided Workers: The Historical Transformation of Labour in the United States* (Cambridge: Cambridge University Press, 1982); Marglin, S. A., 'What do bosses do? The origins and functions of hierarchy in capitalist production', *Review of Radical Political Economics*, Vol. 6 (1974) pp. 33–60.
13. McPherson (1983) (see note 6).
14. Williamson (1980) (see note 3).

15. *Report of the Committee of Inquiry under Professor E. H. Phelps Brown into Certain Matters Concerning Labour in Building and Civil Engineering*, Cmnd. 3714 (HMSO, 1968) p. 22.
16. Leopold, E., 'Where have all the workers gone?', *Building*, Vol. 243 (22 October 1982), pp. 29–38.
17. Casson, M. C., *The Firm and the Market* (Oxford: Basil Blackwell, 1987) Chapter 6.
18. Villa, P., 'Labour Market Segmentation in the Construction Industry in Italy', in Wilkinson, F. (ed.), *The Dynamics of Labour Market Segmentation* (London: Academic Press, 1981).
19. Keating, B. P., 'Standards: implicit, explicit and mandatory', *Economic Inquiry*, Vol. 19 (1981) pp. 449–58.
20. Casson (1987) (see note 17).
21. Moore, R., 'Aspects of segmentation in the United Kingdom building industry labour market', in Wilkinson, F. (ed.), *The Dynamics of Labour Market Segmentation* (London: Academic Press, 1981).
22. Gabriel, J. and Holzapfl, F., 'Entrepreneurial strategies of adjustment and internal labour markets' in Wilkinson, F. (ed.), *The Dynamics of Labour Market Segmentation* (London: Academic Press, 1981).
23. Villa (1981) (see note 18).
24. Moore (1981) (see note 21).
25. Arighi, G., 'A Crisis of Hegemony', in Amin, S. *et al.*, *Dynamics of Global Crisis* (London: Macmillan, 1982).
26. Hillebrandt, P. M., *Analysis of the British Construction Industry* (London: Macmillan, 1984) p. 213.
27. Bain, G. S. (ed.), *Industrial Relations in Britain* (Oxford: Basil Blackwell, 1983).
28. Bain, G. S. and Elsheikh, F., 'An inter-industry analysis of unionization in Britain', *British Journal of Industrial Relations*, Vol. 17 (1979), pp. 127–57.
29. Department of Employment *Employment Gazette* (January 1986), p. 18 and May 1988, p. 277.
30. McCormick, B. J., 'Trade union reaction to Technological Change in the Construction Industry', *Yorkshire Bulletin of Economic and Social Research*, Vol. 16, No. 12 (1964) pp. 15–30.
31. McCarthy, W. E. J., *The Closed Shop in Britain* (Oxford: Basil Blackwell, 1964).
32. Dunn, S. and Gennard, J., *The Closed Shop in British Industry* (London: Macmillan, 1984) pp. 16–19.
33. Smith, C. T. B. *et al.*, *Strikes in Britain*, Department of Employment Manpower Series No. 15 (London: HMSO, 1978).
34. Hillebrandt (1984) (see note 26).
35. CSO *Monthly Digest of Statistics* No. 507 (March 1988) (London: HMSO, 1988) Table 3.13.
36. McCormick (1964) (see note 30).
37. Department of Environment, Housing and Construction Statistics 1971–81 (London: HMSO, 1982) Table 23. Department of Environment, Housing and Construction Statistics 1976–86 (London: HMSO 1987) Table 2.7.

38. International Labour Organisation *Yearbook of Labour Statistics 1987* (Geneva: ILO, 1987).

39. See Foster, H. G., 'Industrial Relations in Construction: 1970–77', *Industrial Relations*, Vol. 17 (1978) pp. 1–17 and Mills, D. Q., 'Construction', in Somers, G. C. (ed.), *Collective Bargaining: Contemporary American Experience* (Wisconsin: IRRA, 1980).

40. Mills (1980) (see note 39).

41. Foster (1978) (see note 39).

42. Mandelstamm, A. B., 'The Effects of Unions on Efficiency in the Residential Construction Industry: A Case Study', *Industrial and Labor Relations Review*, Vol. 18 (1965) pp. 503–21.

43. Haber, W. and Levinson, H., *Labor Relations and Productivity in the Building Trades* (Ann Arbor: University of Michigan, 1956).

44. Hanson, C., Jackson, S. and Miller, D., *The Closed Shop* (Aldershot: Gower, 1982).

45. Shulenburger, D. E., 'A Contour Theoretic Approach to the Determination of Negotiated Wage Change in the Building Construction Industry', *Economic Inquiry*, Vol. 16 (1978) pp. 395–419.

46. Lipsky, D. B. and Farber, H. S., 'The Composition of Strike Activity in the Construction Industry', *Industrial and Labor Relations Review* Vol. 29 (1976) pp. 388–404.

47. Mills (1980) (see note 39).

48. Villa (1981) (see note 18).

49. Williamson (1980) (see note 3).

50. Casson (1987) (see note 17).

51. Whelchel, B. D., 'Informal Bargaining in Construction', *Industrial Relations*, Vol. 10 (1971) pp. 105–9.

52. Codrington, C. and Henley, J. S., 'The industrial relations of injury and death: safety representatives in the construction industry', *British Journal of Industrial Relations*, Vol. 19 (1981) pp. 297–315.

53. Bowlby, R. L., Carroll, S. L. and Evans, R., 'Measuring the social costs of instability in construction', *Monthly Labor Review*, Vol. 103 (1980) pp. 53–7.

54. These are dealt with in Chapter 4 of this volume as well as in Buckley and Casson (1976) (1985) (see note 3) and Dunning, J. H., *International Production and the Multinational Enterprise* (London: Allen & Unwin, 1981).

55. Casson (1987) (see note 17).

56. Casson (1987) (see note 17).

57. Neo, R. B., *International Construction Contracting* (Aldershot: Gower, 1976).

58. Seymour, H., Flanagan, R., and Norman, G., 'International investment in the construction industry: an application of the eclectic approach', unpublished paper (1985).

59. Lecraw, D., 'Third world multinationals in the service industries', in Enderwick, P. (ed.), *Multinational Service Industries* (London: Croom Helm, 1986).

60. Wells, L. T., 'Third World Multinationals (Cambridge, Mass: MIT Press, 1983).

61. US Department of Commerce, *US Service Industries in World Markets: Current Problems and Future Policy Development*, Washington D. C. (1976).
62. Barna, T., 'Process plant contracting: a competitive new European industry', in Shepherd, G., Duchene, F. and Saunders, C. (eds), *Europe's Industries: Public and Private Strategies for Change* (London: Frances Pinter, 1983).
63. Neo (1976) (see note 57).

Editors' Bridging Commentary

Chapter 9 links back to most of the earlier chapters. Like the product itself, pricing policy in the construction industry is complex for a number of reasons, most of them related to the process itself.

Chapter 9 sets out in a rigorous manner those aspects of probability and economic theory which assist in explaining how the pricing mechanism operates in the industry. The environment in which construction firms operate is one where risk and uncertainty prevail on both the demand and supply sides, and the chapter underlines how different contractual arrangements may shift the balance of risk between client and contractor and the importance of the availability and proper costing of resources, including management. A sound pricing policy is the *sine qua non* for the achievement of business objectives in specific markets and in the long run is crucial to the success of the firms' financial strategy.

9 Pricing Policy

Roger Flanagan and George Norman

9.1 INTRODUCTION

The objective of this chapter is to outline the economic principles underlying price determination in the building industry. The focus is drawn in a deliberately narrow way in that it is concerned solely with price determination of a complete building project rather than that of individual components or elements of a building. However, many of the principles identified apply as much to subcontractors as to main contractors.

Simple economic propositions on price determination do not apply in the building industry. Perfectly competitive conditions are conspicuous by their absence; oligopoly or (contestable) monopoly are much more relevant market structures. Risk and uncertainty are endemic both in the projection of work load (demand) and of costs (supply). The competitive processes by which building projects are awarded are price guided, but in ways that generally are not treated in the simple economics textbooks; competitive tendering, negotiated tenders, etc. are rarely considered in economic analysis of 'the price system'.

This does not mean to say that price determination in the building industry is somehow 'outside' economics. What it does imply is that rather more complicated economic models are needed that take explicit account of the imperfectly competitive environment in which clients and contractors operate.

Section 9.2 outlines the basic principles of pricing behaviour and identifies the major determinants of price. The conclusion of this section is that, other things being equal, the price level will be crucially dependent upon the cost estimation process and the allocation of risk. These are considered in Section 9.3. Empirical evidence relating to a commonly used pricing system is presented in Section 9.4, analysed in the light of the discussion in Section 9.2, and Section 9.5 presents the main conclusions.

9.2 PRICING SYSTEMS IN THE BUILDING INDUSTRY

There is a wide variety of pricing systems in use in the building industry, related in the main to the contractual arrangements made between client and contractor. The main types of contractual arrangements are as follows:[1]

1. Design–Build (package deal, turnkey)
2. Design–Bid with contractor completing part of the design–build
3. Lump sum fixed price
4. Lump sum fluctuating price
5. Schedule of rates, remeasured on completion
6. Management fee contracting with guaranteed maximum price and a fixed management fee
7. Management fee contracting with a target price and a fixed management fee
8. Management fee contracting with a target price and a fluctuating management fee
9. Cost reimbursement
10. Construction management with separate trade contracts (contractor or professional consultant) with trades bid upon a fixed lump sum
11. Construction management with separate trade contracts, with trades on cost reimbursement

So far as price determination is concerned, two distinguishing features of the contractual arrangements are important:

1. The selection and number of contractors competing for the particular project
2. Whether the initially quoted price can be negotiated between client and contractor prior to the final award of the contract

These features allow the construction of the matrix in Figure 9.1 in which is illustrated the economic 'model' appropriate to the particular combination of features and typical forms of contract to which they apply.

The most relevant models for the building industry are A, B and D in Figure 9.1. It is highly unlikely that a client would call for a bid from a single contractor without the option of subsequent negotiation: about the only situation in which this is likely to arise is where contractor and client belong to the same organisation – e.g., where contractor and developer are subsidiaries of the same corporation (see C in Figure 9.1).

Negotiation		
	Yes	*No*
One	Bilateral/ Contestable monopoly A Negotiated tender with single contractor	(Contestable) monopoly C Contractor within same group
Several	Auction with rebid B Negotiated competitive tender: two-stage tender	Sealed bid auction D Competitive tender; lump sum bid

(Left side label: **Number of competing contractors**)

Figure 9.1 Economic models and building contracts

9.2.1 Sealed bid auctions

Traditionally, building work has most commonly been awarded on the basis of competitive tenders without negotiation (Box D in Figure 9.1), and it is this type of contractual arrangement which is dealt with in this section. It is, in fact, the case that despite the relative neglect of auctioning processes as pricing systems in the economics textbooks, the practice of allocating resources by means of some competitive bidding or auction process is widespread: it ranges from open auctions of works of art or property to sealed bid auctions of oil exploration rights or construction contracts. It is only in recent years, however, that a coherent body of theory has been developed in which the pricing and efficiency implications of this method of resource allocation have been examined.[2]

The most common application of the theory of sealed bid auctions is to the investigation of competitive bidding for offshore petroleum leases.[3] Assume that there are N bidders, each of whom is considering submitting a sealed tender for an item, which for convenience might be taken as the right to explore for and exploit oil reserves in a particular offshore tract. The tract is awarded to the bidder who submits the highest bid. It is assumed that the tract is of unknown true value V but that each bidder receives some indication of what the true value might be (e.g., on the basis of seismic reports on oil reserves in neighbouring tracts). On the basis of this information bidder i forms an estimate V_i of the true value, where it is assumed that V_i is a random variable and is an independently distributed, unbiased estimate of V. It is easy to show that the bidder should not submit a bid equal to his estimate V_i. Consider the case in which there is only one bidder. If that bidder does submit a bid equal to his estimate, the expected value of his profit is zero. Matters are made even worse if the bidder is in competition with other bidders. Bidders are now subject to what has come to be known as the 'winner's curse'.[4] The tract will be allocated to the bidder who most over-estimates its true value, and expected profits will be negative. As a consequence, it seems more reasonable to assume that each bidder will bid some fraction v_i of his estimate V_i.[5]

How can this theory be applied to competitive tendering in the building industry? There is, in fact, a direct analogy between the two bidding processes. The item being 'auctioned' is now a building contract of unknown true cost C. Tenderers form estimates C_i of that true cost on the basis of information derived from bills of quantities, drawings and specifications, any nominated elements of the contract, and from previous experience of similar contracts. They can be expected to submit a tender that incorporates some mark-up c_i of the estimated cost[6] C_i since, once again, there is a winner's curse if contractors submit bids equal to their estimates: the contract is likely to be awarded to that tenderer who most underestimates the true cost of the contract, leading to negative expected profit. Table 9.1 summarises the main elements of this analogy.

Table 9.1 Analogy between bidding for oil exploration leases and building contracts

Oil exploration	Building contract
True value: V	True cost: C
Information: Seismic reports; neighbouring leases.	Information: Bills of Quantities (B.Q.); similar contracts; specialist subcontractors and material suppliers' prices
Estimated value: V_i	Estimated cost: C_i
Bid fraction: v_i	Bid mark up: c_i
Bid submitted: $P_i = v_i V_i$	Bid submitted: $P_i = c_i C_i$
Lease award: high bid	Contract award: low bid

In identifying the optimal mark up, it must be recognised that contractors do not have unlimited resources, nor do they tender on only single contracts. Winning a particular contract will carry implications for the resources available to undertake future contracts. In economic terms, the contractor in formulating a bid for any one contract must, therefore, take into account both the direct costs and the opportunity costs[7] of the contract.

Using the approach of Kortanek, Soden and Sodaro[8] generates the following equation for the optimal bid price.

$$b_k \left[1 + \frac{1}{\epsilon_k(g_k(b_k))} \right] + d_k + \lambda_k(C_k) \tag{9.1}$$

where:

$g_k(b_k)$ = subjective probability of winning contract k with bid price b_k

$\epsilon_k(\ )$ = elasticity of $g_k(b_k)$ with respect to a change in b_k

d_k = direct costs of contract k

$\lambda_k(C_k)$ = opportunity costs of contract k

Equation (9.1) has a standard economic interpretation once it is recognised that $g_k(\ )$ is a form of demand function. The optimal bid price b_k for contract k is that bid price which equates marginal revenue from contract k with marginal (direct and opportunity) cost of contract k: the expression $b_k \dfrac{(1 + 1)}{\epsilon_k(\ )}$ is just marginal revenue.

The pricing equation (9.1) is illustrated in Figure 9.2 on the assumption that $g_k(b_k)$ is continuous and concave.[9] Any price above β_k has no chance of winning. Given the cost and market conditions illustrated in Figure 9.2, the optimal bid price is $b_k{}^*$.

It is of interest to investigate the effects on optimal bid price of a change in the environment in which the contractor is bidding. This will be treated relatively briefly here.[10] Three of the appealing intuitive results that follow from equation (9.1) are that optimal bid price for a particular contractor falls with an increase in the number of contractors invited to tender, rises with an increase in work load of the contractor, and falls with the quality of information made available to contractors.

Now consider a more complicated situation in which the tender list

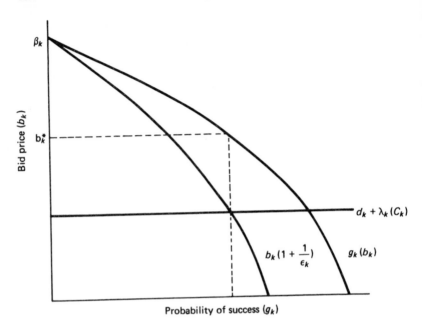

Figure 9.2 Optimal bid price

may contain contractors of sharply differing efficiency. Consider Case A, in Figure 9.3, in which all contractors invited to tender for a particular project have wide experience of similar projects and of local factors likely to influence the project (e.g., ground conditions). Contrast this with Case B, in Figure 9.3, in which the tender list is much more diverse and includes contractors with little direct knowledge of the type or location of the project.

It is to be expected that the maximum bid price β^A_k for Case A will be lower than that, β^B_k for case B. It follows, as intuition would suggest, that the optimal bid prices will be lower in Case A than in Case B (see Figure 9.3).

A rather more subtle point emerges from this analysis that is most easily demonstrated by means of the, admittedly extreme, example illustrated in Figure 9.4. Assume that the tender list for a building contract k contains only two bidders:

1. Contractor 1, a highly efficient contractor with extensive knowledge of previous contracts similar to contract k;

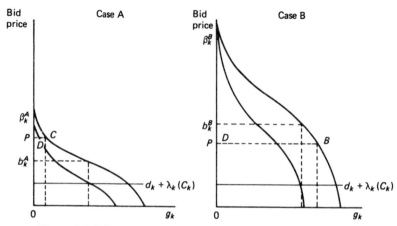

Figure 9.3 Effect on bid price of differing contractor efficiency

2. Contractor 2, a relatively inefficient contractor with little previous experience of this type of work.

It is thus assumed that the direct and opportunity costs for contract k are lower for contractor 1 than for contractor 2. It is also to be expected that the probability of success curve for contractor 1 will lie above that for contractor 2. Contractor 1, for example, knows that he is relatively efficient and experienced in contracts of type k, and so would expect a higher probability of success at any bid price b_k than would contractor 2. The outcome of this tender competition is indeterminate. It is perfectly conceivable, as illustrated in Figure 9.4, that the contract will be won by the inexperienced, higher cost contractor.

The highly simplified analysis of Figure 9.4 leads to rather more general conclusions. First, a tender list that is drawn up without attention being paid to the relative efficiencies and experience of the contractors is likely to lead to the client paying a higher price. In addition, there is at least some possibility that the contract will be won by a relatively inefficient and inexperienced contractor. Finally, note that, as can be seen from Figure 9.4, the inefficient contractor applies a relatively low mark up. If such a contractor wins the tender competition the client is exposed to greater risk. These conclusions lead to the further implication that pre-tender interviews with potential contractors are likely to generate more competitive prices and reduce the risk exposure of the client. These interviews will obviate

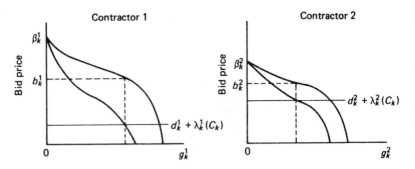

Figure 9.4 Contractors of differing efficiencies

problems that will arise in selecting an inexperienced contractor, or one who has a heavy current work load.

9.2.2 Negotiated bids

An increasing proportion of building contracts is awarded on the basis of negotiation at some stage between client and contractor. It probably remains true that this negotiation occurs subsequent to the contractor being chosen on the basis of a competitive tender; contractors are unlikely to be willing to allow the client the possibility of 'playing off' one contractor against another. The distinction between *tendering* in this case and 'conventional' tendering on a lump sum bid lies in the pre-tender information made available to contractors and the allocation of contract responsibilities between client and contractor. These issues affect the contractor's estimates of cost and evaluation of risk – and so the opportunity costs to which reference was made in section 9.2.1 – but they do not affect the fundamental pricing equation developed above. They are considered in more detail in Section 9.3.

The process of *negotiation* itself warrants attention as a determinant of the final contract price. Effectively there is now a bilateral monopoly (box A in Figure 9.1): a single buyer (the client) facing a single seller (the selected contractor). Both will have identified a price range within which they are willing to negotiate. For the client, the upper limit of this range is determined by the benefits (evaluated in some financial terms) the building is expected to generate and an evaluation of the worth of the managerial services the contractor is expected to provide. The lower limit is much less precise, relating to what is felt by the client to be the minimum price the contractor is likely to accept while still providing a satisfactory service.

For the contractor, the lower limit is determined by his evaluation of the costs (direct and opportunity) he will incur and the risks he will have to accept. The upper limit is a more subjective estimate of what he feels the client would be willing to pay rather than pull out of the contract or enter into negotiation with another contractor.

The potential for an equilibrium price being identified depends upon the extent to which these two price ranges overlap. Thus, in the case illustrated in Figure 9.5(a) there is little probability of successful negotiation, while Figure 9.5(b) should generate an equilibrium price.

There remains the question, of course, of where the equilibrium price will fall. No definitive answer is possible, the outcome being dependent upon the distribution of knowledge, risk and power between the participants in the negotiation: client and contractor. Some qualitative statements can, however, be made. The appropriate economic model, as noted above, is bilateral monopoly. From the client's perspective, the desire is for a low price consistent with the project being completed on time, to specification and with the

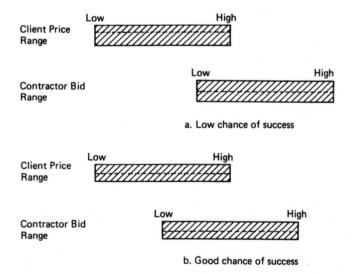

Figure 9.5 Negotiation
a Low chance of success
b Good chance of success

minimum of contractual claims. His power in the negotiation will be determined by the quality of professional advice he receives, his own experience as a client of the building industry and, by implication, whether the project under consideration is 'one-off' or part of a regular building programme.

From the contractor's perspective, the desire is to find a competitive price that is consistent with an acceptable rate of return, given the risk and uncertainties inherent in the construction process. Again a distinction has to be drawn between 'one-off' and regular clients of the industry. In addition, and related to this, the contractor must take into account the extent to which the client has committed himself to a single contractor. The less experienced the client, the more he is committed to the contractor, and the poorer his professional advice, the greater is the contractor's relative power.

The lower the degree to which the client is committed, and the more frequently the client commissions building work, the more the relevant economic model shades from bilateral monopoly into a contestable market – and a contestable monopoly.[11]

The essential feature of contestable markets is that there exist potential suppliers of that market who can enter *and leave* the market relatively costlessly. If too high a price is charged by incumbent firms a potential entrant will come in, undercut the incumbents and so take part of the market, then leave once price has been competed down. Any incumbent firm is, therefore, severely constrained in its pricing policy by the threat of such *potential* entry.

These principles can be applied to building contracts allocated by tender and subsequent negotiation. Those invited to tender incur costs in preparation of the tender documents, but these costs are a relatively small proportion of total costs on a new project, and can be treated as sunk costs on an existing project. In other words, entry to and exit from negotiation is relatively costless. Thus, while the selected contractor is effectively in a monopoly position at the negotiation stage in that he faces no competition from other contractors *within* the negotiation, he does face potential competition from other contractors in two ways if he pushes for too high a price. First, the client may decide to withdraw from the negotiation and appoint another contractor. Secondly, the client may choose not to appoint this contractor on future projects, but rather to go to one of his competitors.

This does not imply that experienced clients will always negotiate the lowest prices. Rather, it implies that they should obtain a more favourable combination of price, delivery and other more subjective measures of quality.

9.3 RISK AND UNCERTAINTY

The discussion of Section 9.2 has alluded to the risks and uncertainties faced by contractors in pricing building projects but has paid little explicit attention to them. This was quite deliberate, since the economic principles upon which price is determined are independent of risk and uncertainty. The determination of the *actual* price is, however, crucially affected by these factors. There are many ways in which tenders can be constructed. In order to make this discussion more precise the discussion concentrates upon estimating and tendering for building work based upon drawings and bills of quantities prepared in accordance with the Standard Method of Measurement of Building Work.

A bill of quantities contains both quantitative and descriptive information with respect to a proposed project. Its purpose is to convey to the tenderer the scope, size and specification of the proposed project to enable a realistic tender to be submitted by the contractor. The information contained in the bill is such that the items are both quantitative and qualitative; they do not portray the construction sequence nor the method of working. It is important to recognise that while the bill items are based upon the known drawn and specification information available to the quantity surveyor at the design stage, inevitably there will be other information about which the contractor must make assumptions when preparing the estimate and the tender – e.g., ground conditions beyond those shown in the trial borehole reports.

From the characteristics found in a typical bill of quantities a number of points emerge:

(a) The contractor is concerned with his financial risk exposure, one important source of risk being that he will be unable to complete the work within the quoted price. The greatest risk will lie in those items that have been priced by the contractor without using quotations from subcontractors or suppliers. A major advantage in the use of subcontractors so far as the main contractor is concerned is that he can pass much of the risk on the the subcontractor.

(b) There will be uncertainty associated with assumptions the contractor has been required to make, for example with respect to expected ground conditions, or the impact of inclement weather on the duration of the project.

(c) Costs will be priced on a unit price basis, but will in fact be some mixture of costs that are:

- Fixed
- Quantity related
- Time related
- Value related
- Project related
- Company related

The details of these relationships are lost when they are subsumed into unit price rates.

(d) The bill of quantities cannot display the technical complexity of the project, nor can it easily give an indication of the buildability of the project. All bills must be examined in conjunction with the drawings if the contractor is to determine the most appropriate method of construction.

(e) If the bill contains a substantial proportion of prime cost and provisional sums the contractor's level of financial risk exposure is reduced, but the limited amount of information available about the sequence and overlapping of work packages will add greater uncertainty to the tender planning process.

(f) The contractor is interested in the sequence of work packages, the continuity and repetition of the activities, the degree of interdependence of trades and operations, the extent of possible mechanisation, and the location of measured items. There is a considerable amount of work involved in converting the drawings and the information in the bill of quantities into a suitable format for estimating. Much of the work will be priced in an operational format and converted into unit price rates.

The estimating process involves estimators, planning engineers, buyers, quantity surveyors, construction engineers, construction and site managers and a number of specialist staff both from within and outside a contractor's organisation. Within the tender preparation period (normally 2–4 weeks) there is a considerable exchange of information, with each of the participants involved interpreting and using the data in some fashion.

Since the estimating process is complex and interrelated, representing the process as a data flow diagram is of some benefit. A data
flow diagram is a network representation of a system, where the system may be automated, manual, or mixed. The data flow diagram portrays the system in terms of its component parts, with all interfaces among the components indicated. It presents the system from the viewpoint of the data rather than from the viewpoint of a person or organisation.

A data flow diagram has four main components:

1. *Data flows*: represented by named vectors (e.g., subcontractors' prices).
2. *Files*: represented by straight lines with a file reference.
3. *Processes*: represented by bubbles.
4. *Data sources and sinks*[12]: represented by boxes.

A data flow diagram should not be confused with a network or precedence diagram which it visually resembles because its objective – namely to look at the pattern of data flowing through a system – is quite different.

The estimating and tendering process is illustrated in the data flow diagram of Figure 9.6, using a model constructed on the basis of interviews with estimators.

Several important points emerge from this flow diagram:

1. The number of different parties involved and the flows of information make the estimating process very complex.
2. Because of the tight time constraint much of the work must be undertaken in parallel; the construction planner will be examining time–cost trade-offs while the subcontractors are preparing estimates for their work packages. Much of the work will be priced by subcontractors, hence the selection of the subcontractors becomes a critically important function.
3. One of the critical pinch points identified by Figure 9.6 is the lack of data on duration and the sequence of work provided to the subcontractor. The tender planner will be working in parallel with the subcontractor; whilst the subcontractor prices the work from the measured and drawn information, the planner is considering the sequence and duration. The system does not provide sufficient time for the planner to complete his work prior to the subcontractor completing his pricing.

142

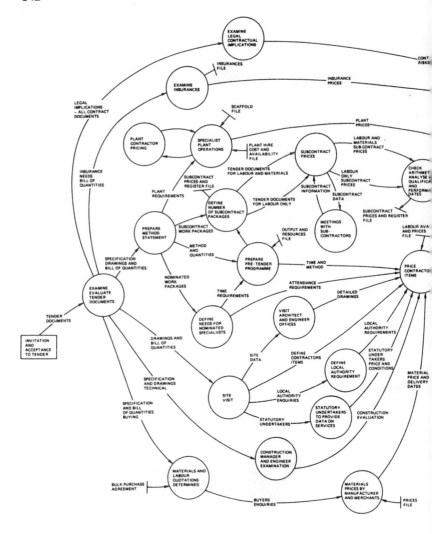

Figure 9.6 Estimating and tendering data flow diagram

Notes: Drawings, BofQ – Drawings, specification and bills of quantities.
Insurance needs – Contractual Insurance requirements, minimum item to cover.
Insurance prices – Price required by insurers to effect cover on contract, limits
of liability.

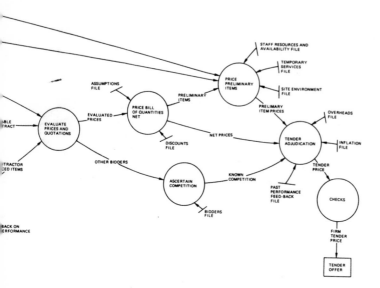

EVALUATE PRICES AND QUOTATIONS

ASSUMPTIONS FILE

PRICE BILL OF QUANTITIES NET

EVALUATED PRICES

PRELIMINARY ITEMS

PRICE PRELIMINARY ITEMS

STAFF RESOURCES AND AVAILABILITY FILE

TEMPORARY SERVICES FILE

SITE ENVIRONMENT FILE

PRELIMINARY ITEM PRICES

OVERHEADS FILE

TENDER ADJUDICATION

NET PRICES

INFLATION FILE

DISCOUNTS FILE

OTHER BIDDERS

ASCERTAIN COMPETITION

KNOWN COMPETITION

TENDER PRICE

PAST PERFORMANCE FEED-BACK FILE

CHECKS

BIDDERS FILE

FIRM TENDER PRICE

TENDER OFFER

ABLE TRACT

NTRACTOR CED ITEMS

BACK ON ERFORMANCE

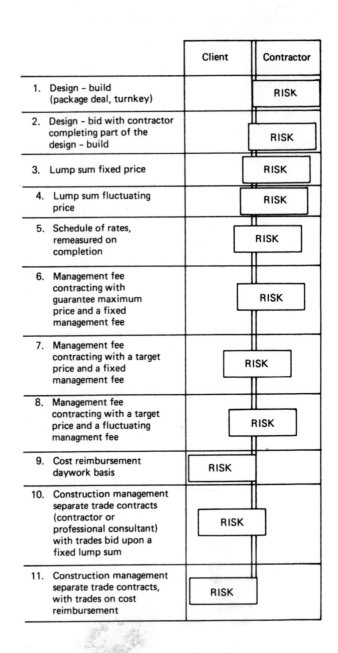

	Client	Contractor
1. Design – build (package deal, turnkey)		RISK
2. Design – bid with contractor completing part of the design – build		RISK
3. Lump sum fixed price		RISK
4. Lump sum fluctuating price		RISK
5. Schedule of rates, remeasured on completion	RISK	
6. Management fee contracting with guarantee maximum price and a fixed management fee	RISK	
7. Management fee contracting with a target price and a fixed management fee	RISK	
8. Management fee contracting with a target price and a fluctuating managment fee	RISK	
9. Cost reimbursement daywork basis	RISK	
10. Construction management separate trade contracts (contractor or professional consultant) with trades bid upon a fixed lump sum	RISK	
11. Construction management separate trade contracts, with trades on cost reimbursement	RISK	

Figure 9.7 Allocation of risk

4. Decisions made about the number of subcontract work packages and the number of subcontract quotations for each work package are major pinch points in the data flow diagram.
5. The subcontractor's pricing process is central to the overall pricing process.

One element implicit in this discussion but not yet dealt with is the allocation of risk between client and contractor. This is not independent of the contractual arrangements, as can be seen from Figure 9.7. The impact on price of the different contractual arrangements is awkward to specify since this impact is not independent of the competitive environment. As the industry has become more competitive in recent years there has been a move to management fee and design–build forms of contract, with demand for a guaranteed maximum price. Nevertheless, it can be stated that the greater the risk imposed on the contractor, the greater the price the client must accept. In other words, the client has to trade off price and risk in the choice of contractual arrangement.

9.4 AN EMPIRICAL ANALYSIS OF COMPETITIVE TENDERING

Data has been collected on some 1 500 building contracts that were put out to competitive tender in 1982–3. This data was classified by CI/SfB code and gives for each contract the descriptive details of the project, project type, location, the client, the list of contractors tendering for the project, and the tender prices.

The theory presented in Section 9.2 would suggest that the quality of bids received, as measured perhaps by the variability of bids, will improve with experience and ability of the contractors tendering. Unfortunately, no direct measure of experience and ability is available. Size of contract can, however, be used as a surrogate if it can be argued that, for example, small inexperienced contractors are unlikely to be invited to tender on large contracts. Further investigation of the tendering data revealed that tender lists on larger projects did, indeed, tend to contain contractors with extensive experience of constructing large scale projects, whereas the tender lists for smaller contracts tended to be rather more diverse.

Figures 9.8(a) and 9.8(b) illustrate histograms describing the distribution of bids received on a total of 116 office projects: each bid

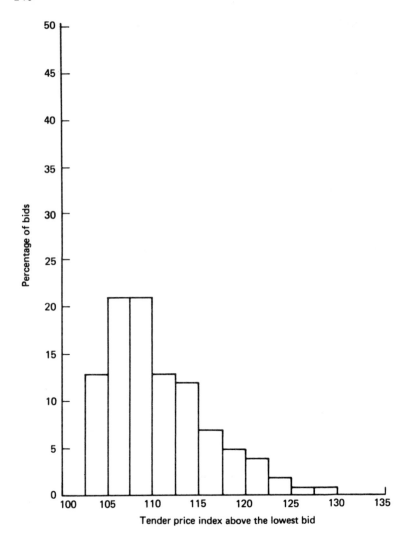

Figure 9.8 a Distribution of bids for office projects under £1 million
Note: Based on 60 projects; lowest bid indexed to 100

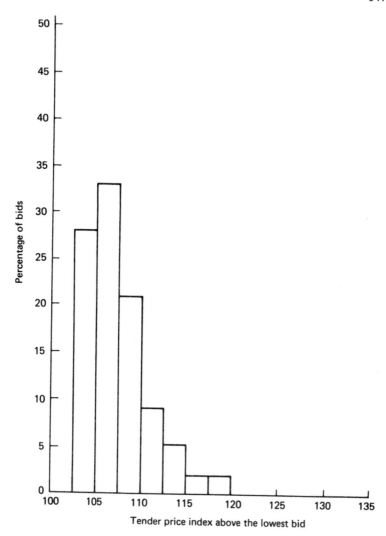

Figure 9.8 b Distribution of bids for office projects over £1 million
Note: Based on 56 projects; lowest bid indexed to 100

is expressed as a percentage above the appropriate low bid (the low bids are excluded). As can be seen, tenders are much 'tighter' on the larger contracts[13]: more than 80 per cent of all tenders on contracts over £1million were within 10 per cent of the low bid, compared to less than 60 per cent for contracts less than £1million.

This analysis is extended in Figures 9.9 and 9.10 to look firstly in more detail at tendering on the office projects and secondly to compare tendering on office projects with that on housing projects. Figures 9.9 and 9.10 use cumulative frequency curves: the further to

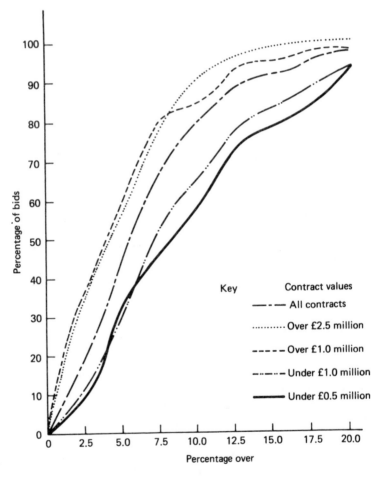

Figure 9.9 Size of contract – office buildings

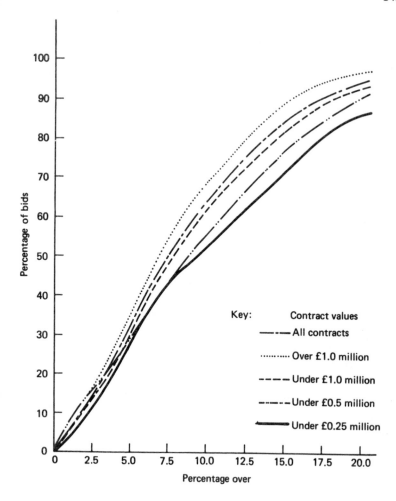

Figure 9.10 Size of contract – housing

the left the curve lies the more concentrated are bids near to the low bid. These graphs support the hypothesis that bids become more concentrated with an increase in job size. In addition, there is a clear indication that this improvement in bid variability is greater for offices than for housing. This is to be expected since there are fewer building contractors capable of undertaking major office projects than there are contractors undertaking housing projects.

Similar comments apply to the results summarised in equation

(9.2). In this case, the logarithm of the bid variance has been regressed against the logarithm of the low bid for a sample of 32 housing contracts. If there is no change in bid variance with contract size a slope coefficient of 2 would be expected (since variance increases as the square of size). As can be seen, the slope coefficient (1.690) is significantly less than 2, implying that tenders are less variable on large contracts:

$$LV = 3.717 + 1.690 \, LLB \, (R^2 = 0.727 : N = 32) \qquad (9.2)$$
$$ (9.242) \quad (8.939)$$

where LV = logarithm of bid variance
$ LLB$ = logarithm of low bid
$ t$ – statistics are given in brackets

A second data set can throw more light on the effects on tender prices of the information available to tenderers. The data were supplied by quantity surveyors' offices, and provide rather more detailed information than the data set discussed above. In particular, it was possible to identify the amount of each contract that was specified under prime cost and provisional sums. Since the tenderer can take these amounts as given, the greater this proportion, the better the quality of information available to the tenderer, and so the lower should be the tender price variability.

The data set for any one type of building is, unfortunately, small and permits statistical analysis only for offices (with a sample of 11). Equation (9.3) summarises the impact on tender price variability of the number of bidders and the pre-specified proportion of the contract (t-statistics are given in brackets):

$$BCV = 2.352 - 71.44 \, TLBD + 0.566 \, NB$$
$$ (1.541) \quad (0.932) \quad (2.372)$$
$$ - 0.059 \, PPCP \, (R^2 = 0.78, \, N=11) \qquad (9.3)$$
$$ (4.043)$$

where BCV = coefficient of variation of bids
$ TLBD$ = low bid (£m)
$ NB$ = number of bidders
$ PPCP$ = percentage of PC and provisional sums.

The coefficients on NB and $PPCP$ are significant at the 5 per cent and 1 per cent levels respectively. They indicate that tender price variability tends to increase with the number of tenderers but to decrease with the percentage of *PC* and provisional sums. This lends further support to the contention that competitive tendering is more likely to arise from an improvement in information available to tenderers than from an increase in the number of firms invited to tender.

9.5   CONCLUSIONS

Pricing policy in the building industry is complex. The economic principles underlying price determination are more sophisticated, but also less certain, than those that characterise perfect competition. Imperfect competition, imperfect knowledge, risk and uncertainty are endemic to the pricing of building projects.

Nevertheless, economic principles can be identified that allow the analysis of price determination and suggest ways in which the price mechanism might be improved. By far the greatest amount of analysis has focused on competitive tendering, or sealed bid auctions, and it is quite clear from this analysis that tender prices are likely to be more competitive the greater the number, experience and knowledge of those invited to tender.

This might be taken to imply that large tender lists will secure competitive prices. There is, however, little to be gained by having more than about four or five tenderers on any list; an argument that is strengthened when account is taken of the costs imposed on the industry, and presumably passed on to clients, as a result of abortive tendering. Competitive tendering is not costless, either for the client or the prospective tenderers. Discussions with contractors indicate that they expend in the order of 0.7–1 per cent of turnover in the handling and preparation of tender documentation. On any given competition with N tenderers, N-1 have incurred abortive costs. No comparable figures are available for clients, but while clients' costs will be lower than those of contractors, nevertheless costs are incurred in preparing and duplicating the initial call for tenders, and in handling and processing subsequent bids.

Effective competitive tendering is much more likely to be secured, and clients' risks reduced, by careful choice of tenderers, taking into account knowledge of their past experience and performance and current work load. In addition, tenders will be made more competitive by improving the quality of information made available to tenderers. This can be done directly by more detailed pre-tender design, and indirectly by, once again, choosing a tender list with care, for example by pre-tender interviews.

Somewhat different considerations apply in the determination of price when this arises as a consequence of some form of two-stage tender, with the second stage involving direct negotiation between client and contractor. This is now a bilateral monopoly or contestable monopoly world in which price emerges from some more or less well informed 'game' between client and contractor. No definite conclusions can be drawn with respect to the likely outcome of this 'game', dependent as it is upon the allocation of power, knowledge and risk between the negotiating parties.

Indeed, this leads to the final conclusion. Extensive analysis is available on competitive tendering, mainly on lump sum bids. It has also been shown that different contractual arrangements give rise to different allocations of risk between client and contractor. What is now needed is a comparison of prices, delivery and performance, under these different contractual arrangements.

NOTES AND REFERENCES

1. For a more detailed discussion of some of these contractual arrangements see Nahapiet, H. and Nahapiet, J., 'A Comparison of Contractual Arrangements for Building Projects', *Construction Management and Economics*, Vol. 3 (1985) pp. 217–31.

2. For useful surveys see: Engelbrecht-Wiggans, R., 'Auctions and Bidding Models: A Survey', *Management Science*, Vol. 26 No. 2 (1980) pp. 119–42; Flanagan, R. and Norman, G., 'Sealed Bid Auctions: an Application to the Building Industry', *Construction Management and Economics*, Vol. 3, No. 2 (1985) pp. 145–61; Stark, R. M. and Rothkopf, M. H., 'Competitive Bidding: A Comprehensive Bibliography', *Operations Research*, Vol. 27 (1985) pp. 364–90.

3. See for example, Reece, D. K., 'Competitive bidding for offshore petroleum leases', *Bell Journal of Economics*, Vol. 9 (1978) pp. 369–84.

4. See Case, J. H., *Economics and the Competitive Process* (New York: University Press, 1979).

5. See Rothkopf, M. H., 'On multiplicative bidding strategies', *Operations Research*, Vol. 28 (1980) pp. 570–5 for a more detailed discussion.

6. The bid submitted is $c_i C_i$, thus the expected percentage mark-up on costs is $(c_i-1) \times 100\%$.

7. Opportunity cost is the cost of the loss of the opportunity to use resources elsewhere – in this case, to undertake a different contract.

8.   Kortanek, K. D., Soden, J. V. and Sodaro, D., 'Profit Analyses and Sequential Bidding Models', *Management Science*, Vol. 17 (1973) pp. 396–417.
9.   It is sufficient that $g_k(b_k)$ be not too strongly convex.
10. For a more detailed and comprehensive discussion see Flanagan and Norman (1985) (see note 2).
11. See Baumol, W. J., 'Contestable Markets: an Uprising in the Theory of Industry Structure', *American Economic Review*, Vol. 72 (1982) pp. 1–15.
12. A data source is obvious, a data sink is the final destination of the data.
13. The break point of £1million was chosen by visual inspection, but is justified by subsequent statistical testing.

Glossary

Barriers to entry   Hindrances to potential entrants to a market because of economic or non-economic advantages held by existing firms.

Bilateral monopoly   A situation in which a single buyer faces a single seller.

Bill of quantities   List of items to be put in place in a construction project. It is used as a basis for pricing of projects by contractors, and usually forms part of the contract documents. It is used, together with the contractor's prices against each item, in any claims by the contractor for additional work on the contract.

Bounded rationality   Rational choice that allows for the limitations of the knowledge and computational capacity of the decision maker.

Cash flow   The passage of liquid funds into and out of a business.

Contestable markets   Markets in which competitive pressures from potential entrants impose constraints on the behaviour of existing suppliers (see Chapter 1).

Contestable monopoly   Contestable market in which there is only one major supplier.

Debt–equity ratio   Debt–equity ratio, gearing and leverage all embody the same concept, and all three may be used in different senses. The first is, in terms of capital, the ratio of the value of debt to the value of shareholders' assets. The second is the value of debt to assets employed *less* debt. Total debt may be defined to exclude short term debt (such as to trade creditors) but to include bonds and debentures. The third is, in terms of income, the ratio of the income needed to service debt to the total income of the company. The more usual interpretations are the first and second.

Dividend cover   The number of times the dividend declared by a company is covered by the company's earnings.

Equilibrium price   The price level at which the supply of and demand for a commodity are equal.

Equity capital   The ordinary shares of a limited company.

Externalisation   The purchase or sale of a resource outside the firm, as opposed to within the firm.

Firm   This term is used in economic theory to refer to any form of operating unit from a simple proprietorship to a large conglomerate.

Fixed capital   Buildings, plant and machinery and vehicles.

Fixed costs   Costs of any undertaking which do not vary in the short term with the level of output.

Gearing   See Debt–equity ratio.

Human capital   Manpower resources of the firm. The use of this term implies its treatment as an asset which may be enhanced in value, for example by training expenditures.

Information impactedness   The situation in which information relating to a transaction is better known to some parties than to others.

Internalisation   The employment of a resource in-house rather than purchase or sale outside the firm.

Internal labour market(ILM)   The situation where the allocation and pricing of labour occur primarily within the organisation.

Joint venture   An arrangement whereby two or more firms undertake a project as partners.

Leverage   See Debt–equity ratio.

Life cycle theory   This theory argues that a product, a firm, or even an industry, follows a typical pattern through four different phases: introduction, growth, maturity and decline.

Marginal costs   The extra cost of production of one additional unit of output.

Neoclassical economics   A development in economic thinking led by Alfred Marshall (1842–1924) which had, and still has, a profound effect on modern economics. It is basically the traditional approach described in Chapter 1, Section 1.1.

Opportunity cost   The evaluation placed on the most highly valued of the rejected alternatives or opportunities.

Portfolio   In a financial sense, the total of the mix of different investments held. It is often also used to describe the mix of businesses in which the company operates.

Provisional sums   Provisional sums are included in the bill of quantities by the quantity surveyor to cover work which is so uncertain that no definite estimate of cost is possible. In some cases they may cover work whose nature and quantity is unknown; in other cases they cover work whose nature is known but where the quantities are unknown.

Retention ratio   The relationship of the profits retained in the business (that is, not distributed to shareholders) to total profits.

Satisficing   Attaining and being satisfied with a certain level of profit, market share, etc. which is not necessarily the maximum obtainable.

Social costs   The costs to society of action by persons or organisations which are not borne by those responsible for their generation.

Social technology   There are two aspects to social technology: routine and non-routine. In its routine form social technology deals with a continuum of situations which face collaborating individuals. The non-routine form deals with novel situations.

Transaction costs   The costs involved in the process of buying and selling both goods and services, including manpower.

Variable costs   Costs which vary directly with changes in the volume of output.

Working capital   The net liquid resources for the day to day operations of a business – that is, in accounting terms, current assets *less* current liabilities.

Appendix
Contents of the Companion Volume,
The Modern Construction Firm

Subject Index

Index of Names